The Conant Controversy
in Teacher Education

Studies in Education

Consulting Editor: Paul Nash, BOSTON UNIVERSITY

The
Conant
Controversy
in Teacher
Education

Robert M. Weiss

STATE UNIVERSITY OF NEW YORK, COLLEGE AT CORTLAND

RANDOM HOUSE   NEW YORK

ACKNOWLEDGMENTS

"The Famous Twenty-Seven" by James D. Conant. *Phi Delta Kappan*, June 1964. By permission of *Phi Delta Kappan*.

"Dr. Conant and his Critics" by Lindley J. Stiles. *Teachers College Record*, May 1964. By permission of *Teachers College Record* and the author.

"Future Implications and Repercussions of the Report" by Harold Taylor. *Freedom with Responsibility in Teacher Education*, Seventeenth Yearbook (1964) of the American Association of Colleges for Teacher Education. By permission of the American Association of Colleges for Teacher Education and the author.

"NSCTE Leaders Discuss Dr. Conant's Views." By permission of John S. Brubacher, Erret Hummel, Everett J. Kircher, Franklin Parker, Gerald H. Read, Howard E. Tempero, and Sloan R. Wayland, participants in the February 1964 National Society of College Teachers of Education panel session.

"Conant's Fight for Better Teaching" by Merle Borrowman. *Atlantic Monthly*, April 1965. Copyright © 1965, by The Atlantic Monthly Co., Boston, Massachusetts. By permission of the publisher and the author.

"Is *The Education of American Teachers* Influencing the Education of American Teachers?" *Phi Delta Kappan*, June 1964. By permission of *Phi Delta Kappan*.

Preface

Many persons contributed to this book. I am especially grateful to those whose views I have tried to represent and evaluate.

Above all, James Bryant Conant is to be thanked. His report, *The Education of American Teachers* (1963), spurred the largest dispute our society has ever had on that subject. The controversy laid bare not only his own but also other approaches to educating American teachers. Due to Conant's enormous effectiveness in provoking response, competing philosophies of teacher education can now be delineated more readily, examined more openly, and evaluated more explicitly. Whether or not one agrees with Conant's ideas and orientation, he deserves immense appreciation for his deep commitment, which has led to a lifetime of extensive and significant endeavors to improve American education and society. He was also kind enough to grant me an interview when I first began this project, but his policy is not to comment regarding manuscripts about him or his views until after their publication.

The selection of material for use in this book was a complex matter. Diverse criteria were employed. I initially obtained permission to insert Conant's chapter on

"The Theory and Practice of Teaching." I later omitted it because of space limitations and because of its wide availability in the 1963 hardcover and the 1964 paperback edition of *The Education*. For the same reasons, I did not insert any of Conant's three later speeches on that subject before national professional organizations. He added those talks to the 1964 paperback to make that a "new, enlarged edition." As Chapter 2 in this book, I used the *Phi Delta Kappan* reprint of Conant's recommendations in *The Education* because that article also contained a later brief but relevant comment by Conant. Phi Delta Kappa is a men's professional society in education; its journal, *Phi Delta Kappan*, contains some of the most stimulating articles on contemporary educational issues to be found in any professional periodical.

I deliberately attempted to balance the selections favorable and unfavorable to Conant's views. I hope to produce and help induce as equitable an evaluation as possible of Conant's teacher education positions and of the other viewpoints his book elicited. In the midst of the controversy, responses to Conant's proposals became polarized into either supportive or critical camps. There were few objective assessments of both the strengths and weaknesses of Conant's teacher education approach. The controversy was highly emotional. This prompted Hendrik D. Gideonse, then chairman of the education department at Bowdoin College and now with the U.S. Office of Education, to question (*Saturday Review*, September 19, 1964): "Is Enlightened Debate Possible?" and to infer that it was then impossible. The passionate dispute has since subsided. I hope that now the issues and the underlying philosophical orientations to educating teachers can and will be examined more rationally. That is one of my objectives in writing this book.

In selecting the pro-Conant articles, I initially planned to incorporate the supporting article by William H. Cartwright of Duke University, and then the accompanying critical one by Harry S. Broudy of the University of Illinois which also appeared in the *Educational Forum* (January 1964). Cartwright has been a consultant to Conant on the teacher education report. These educators had graciously granted me permission to use their articles, but I decided to omit Cartwright's piece because it mostly repeated and only somewhat elaborated on Conant's widely-available statements. I then decided to exclude Broudy's article because it seemed unfair to insert either one without the other when originally they had been published as a pair.

Lindley J. Stiles' article (Chapter 3 in this book) was picked both for its pro-Conant perspective and because it was the only evaluation, though very one-sided, of many of the critical reviews of *The Education*. When Stiles was dean of the School of Education at the University of Wisconsin, he had conflicted with the National Council for the Accreditation of Teacher Education (NCATE) over the "all-university" approach to teacher education which he and Conant favor. Stiles has since become a professor of education for interdisciplinary studies and political science and sociology at Northwestern University, one of the institutions currently conducting an experimental program which grew directly out of Conant's proposals in *The Education*.

For the second pro-Conant selection, Chapter 6, I chose one by Merle Borrowman which appeared in the April 1965 *Atlantic Monthly*. There were many reasons for that choice. Like Stiles, Borrowman is especially qualified to speak on the subject, having also served as a consultant to Conant on *The Education*. In addition, Borrowman is a trained historian of education who has written and edited two books on the history of teacher education. He presently serves as professor of education and history at the University of Wisconsin where he is chairman of the department of educational policies studies. Borrowman has received the rights to direct a multivolume biography of Conant. Borrowman's article was the last full-length one on the subject to appear in a literary periodical, almost two years after *The Education*'s initial release. In Chapter 6, Borrowman cautiously but definitely supports Conant; Borrowman also details and assesses some of the effects of *The Education* and some of Conant's subsequent efforts.

Choosing the anti-Conant articles or speeches was more difficult than the pro-Conant ones. While there were numerous descriptive, unanalytical, popular-newspaper reviews, there were many more critical and analytical professional articles and speeches than noncritical ones. I decided to eliminate those pieces which stressed only a single issue or aspect of the conflict such as the ones by Joe Burnett of the University of Illinois in *Educational Theory* (January 1964) and Richard Seckinger of the University of Pittsburgh in the *History of Education Quarterly* (September 1964). Points from such articles could be easily summarized and incorporated into my own analysis and then these writings could be cited in either the footnotes or the bibliography.

As mentioned, one result of *The Education* was that Conant gave three national addresses in 1964 before four national professional organizations: the American Association of Colleges for Teacher Education

(AACTE); a joint session of the Association for Student Teaching (AST) and the National Society of College Teachers of Education (NSCTE); and before the National Association of Secondary-School Principals (NASSP). These three speeches were the ones added to the 1964 paperback edition of *The Education*. The formal responses to his AACTE talk were published only in the AACTE 1964 yearbook entitled *Freedom and Responsibility in Teacher Education*. In the case of AST-NSCTE, there was a previously unpublished panel discussion by leaders of NSCTE. I decided to choose from those responses to present views critical of those of Conant. Those reactions seemed best to depict the flavor of the controversy, to illustrate the deep conflict of outlooks, and to represent the alternate philosophical approaches to teacher education, and they were also not widely distributed and available. In addition, these 1964 AACTE, AST, and NSCTE conferences took place simultaneously and were the ones which had led Gideonse to express disappointment about the possibilities of rational debate.

There were three different published responses at the 1964 AACTE convention. One was a questionnaire distributed by AACTE which demonstrated that among those polled (probably mostly administrators), there was generally considerable division about Conant's proposals. This indicated that there was not as much unanimity among educationists as might be expected from what Conant had dubbed an "establishment." The two other formal responses at the 1964 AACTE annual meeting were speeches by Frances S. Chase, former dean of the School of Education at the University of Chicago and professor of education there, and by Harold Taylor, former president of Sarah Lawrence University and vice-chairman of the Citizens Committee for Public Schools and director of an AACTE study on teacher education in world affairs.

I decided to include the edited version of the NSCTE panel discussion (Chapter 5) not only because it has never been previously published but also because it contains the reactions of a number of leaders of NSCTE rather than that of merely another single respondent. Neither NSCTE nor any of its sections nor affiliated societies ever took an official position regarding *The Education*. That discussion represents only the individual views of those who were selected to be on the panel. I happened to edit the transcript of the NSCTE panel discussion because I served in 1963–1964 as *NSCTE Newsletter* editor.

The 1964 NSCTE panel chairman was John S. Brubacher, professor of higher education at the Center for the Study of Higher Education at the University of Michigan, 1963–1964 NSCTE President who has coauthored a history of higher education and written two other books on history and philosophy of education. In order of speaking, the other panel members were: Sloan R. Wayland, professor of education at Teachers College, Columbia University, who was 1963–1964 chairman of NSCTE's educational sociology section; Erret Hummel, professor of education at Portland State College, who was 1963–1964 chairman of NSCTE's administration, supervision, and curriculum section; Gerald H. Read, professor of theoretical foundations of education at Kent State University, who was executive secretary-treasurer of the Comparative Education Society; Everett J. Kircher, professor of education at Ohio State University, who served as 1963–1964 chairman of the NSCTE Philosophy of Education Society section;

Howard E. Tempero, professor of educational psychology and measurements at Teachers College, University of Nebraska, who was 1963–1964 chairman of NSCTE's educational psychology section; and Franklin Parker, then professor of education at the University of Oklahoma and currently Benedum Professor of Education at West Virginia University, who was 1963–1964 president of the History of Education Society. Like Borrowman and Stiles, all of the panelists have training and experience which especially qualify them to speak on teacher education.

Because I chose to insert the previously-unpublished NSCTE panel discussion (Chapter 5) and still desired balance among the selections while avoiding repetition, it was necessary to choose between Chase's and Taylor's AACTE talks. Again, both speakers were well qualified to speak on the subject. Both had graciously granted me permission to include their remarks. I finally decided to use Taylor's (Chapter 4) because he has been more prolific and is better known than Chase as a critic of Conant's teacher-education views. Finally, because it has been the only published survey attempting to evaluate qualitatively the impact of *The Education of American Teachers*, I included as Chapter 7 a *Phi Delta Kappan* "listening post" article.

Conversation and some correspondence with Harold Taylor were helpful to me. Taylor was kind enough to read Chapter 1 of the manuscript and make some suggestions. Considerable appreciation for his encouragement and aid as this work went through various stages of development are particularly due Jack Hollister, project administrator at Educational Testing Service of Conant's "A Study of American Education." I am also grateful to Elmer Clark, Warren Baller, John S. Brubacher, and John I. Goodlad, 1965–1966, 1964–1965, 1963–1964, and 1962–1963 presidents of the National Society of College Teachers of Education (NSCTE), for their support of my desire to see this controversy openly and, I hope, objectively assessed in book form. For his cooperation, I also want to thank Edward C. Pomeroy, executive secretary of the American Association of Colleges for Teacher Education (AACTE).

I am indebted to Franklin S. Parker of West Virginia University for his general bibliographical assistance and for graciously sharing his unpublished, revised 1964 compilation of "The Educational Writings of James Bryant Conant." Shirley Guerra of the Austin, Texas Public Schools assisted Professor Parker in the preparation of that bibliography. Appreciation also needs to be expressed to Paul Franklin Douglass of Rollins College, whose *Six Upon the World* (1954) contains the most complete presentation of Conant's life and thought yet published. Unless specifically cited to another source, biographical information about Conant has been taken from the Douglass book. Douglass also graciously offered me further assistance which I did not need. He recently wrote me that he has not found any errors in what he wrote about Conant since *Six Upon the World* was published. I also want to thank Dean B. J. Chandler for providing me with the unpublished transcript of the November 1964 Northwestern Conference on Teacher Education; and James E. Perdue, president of the State University of New York at Oswego, and Roy E. Lieuallen, chancellor of the Oregon State System of Higher Education, for lending me their personal copies of their unpublished doctoral dissertations which related to Conant's views on education.

For initially stimulating me to enter the fields of history and philosophy of education, I will always be indebted to Larry Cremin. I have yet to meet a more devoted and able scholar. For what I have also learned professionally and personally from them, appreciation is due Don Adams, George Axtelle, Marc Berger, Merle Borrowman, Freeman Butts, Jack Childs, George Counts, Frank Durgin, Claude Eggertson, Tom Green, Erling Hunt, Al Loving, Jim McClellan, Paul Nash, Allan Nevins, John Herman Randall, Glen Rasmussen, Bruce Raup, Earle Rugg, Jim Russell, Bill Schulte, Dick Seckinger, and Bill Van Til, as well as many of my students. For additional support of my professional endeavors, I am also indebted to Bill Cruickshank and David French.

The librarians at Cornell University, Harvard University, the New York Public Library, the State University of New York at Cortland, and Syracuse University aided in the research I did for this volume. At Cortland, I should especially like to thank Jim Lee, Bess Purdy, Dorothy Pritchard, and Fred Schuhle.

A dedication would have been to Sandy for her constant love and assistance; to our children, Janet and Steven, for accepting our loss of time together while I worked on this project, and to my parents, Hermina and Edward, for having encouraged me in my educational goals.

For their fine work in compiling and typing, I wish to thank my former secretaries, Janice Bennett and Ann Ottenschot. For their clerical, secretarial, library, and other assistance, I want to express appreciation to Suzanne Brookins, Mrs. Pauline Crawford, Jo Ann Daly, Esther Dewey, Mrs. Margot Fuller, Mrs. Hazel Genton, Kevin Gottlieb, Barbara Metsky, and Mrs. Barbara Wallace.

For encouragement and patience with this endeavor and guidance in its improvement, I wish to thank Robert Weiss, former education editor at Random House who is now with the University of Michigan Press; Leonard H. Roberts, the present editor, and Mrs. Sybil Elman Maimin, the manuscript editor who did an exceptionally fine job of improving upon the accuracy, clarity, and style of the submitted manuscript.

Responsibility for the final work is entirely mine.

R.M.W.

Contents

The Conant Controversy
in Teacher Education

1

Teacher Education
and Dr. Conant

Robert M. Weiss

Published in September 1963, James Bryant Conant's
The Education of American Teachers became the most
widely discussed book on education in the last quarter
of a century. In February 1964, *Parents' Magazine* selected Dr. Conant for its award for "outstanding service
to children" for his many contributions to education including his teacher education study. The following October, the American Council on Education gave him its
book award—a gold medal and one thousand dollars
contributed by the Borden Company Foundation, Inc.
In December, *Saturday Review* designated *The Education* the most important book on education for both
1963 and 1964. All but one of 19 judges chosen by that
periodical included *The Education* on their list of nom-
inations for that two-year award. For reasons that will

become apparent later in this chapter, it should be noted here that second to *The Education*, with the vote of 11 judges, was *Self-Renewal* (1963) by John W. Gardner, president of the Carnegie Corporation of New York, which sponsored *The Education*. (Gardner resigned from the Carnegie Corporation to become U.S. Secretary of Health, Education, and Welfare and subsequently resigned from the government post to return to the Carnegie Corporation.)

The Education of American Teachers prompted the most extensive dispute that American society has had on the subject. Heated commentary continued for over two years after the book's release. On the one hand, Conant's teacher education stands were generally lauded uncritically in the over 2,000 popular reviews of the work. On the other, because Conant challenged much of accepted educational theory, many educationists expressed considerable disagreement with him. The specific controversy has become an affair of the past, but the issues it highlighted persist. One purpose of this book is to delineate the diverse orientations which came to the fore. These still help determine the questions asked and thus, the answers given about teacher education in the United States.

Conant's stated aim was to prepare from a two-year study a single volume in order to introduce the public to the complexity of American teacher education. He also indicated in his preface that he had undertaken *The Education* with some reluctance because of the unsettled nature of the topic. As Conant knew, his work did not cause the concern or the conflicting approaches. It did become the major catalyst in bringing these differences into the open so that the professionals had to face them, even though the public did not. Because

Conant focused special attention on certain issues, respondents frequently treated those as the key ones. While some professionals questioned the priority of Conant's choices, these nevertheless became the bases for many of the substantive replies to the book.

As Merle Borrowman, who was a consultant on the study, has written, "by refusing to argue beyond the point where a fundamental value conflict becomes clear Conant avoids developing hostilities that would make subsequent collaboration difficult or uncomfortable." [1] Yet, Dr. Conant does not shun detailing his opinions for debate by others. By the time he wrote *The Education*, he had decided to make specific recommendations, and he also included general suggestions to be considered, given the implementation of his specific recommendations. The ordering of his proposals into recommendations and suggestions, in that priority, seem to reflect his greater concern with and certainty about those administrative, organizational, and structural matters upon which his recommendations concentrated.

By making specific recommendations, Conant encouraged political action. He also organized the summary of his recommendations according to the various agencies and officials he deemed responsible for implementing them. *The Education* was a political document rather than an intellectual treatise. In Chapter 3 of this book, Lindley J. Stiles defends Conant's political approach. Conant aimed at securing support for his proposals from both professionals and laymen. The Conant controversy in teacher education could be approached as a case study in the politics of education. Conant sought controversy. As he stated in a radio broadcast after publication of *The Education*, which was quoted

in March 1964, "My only worry is that there won't be a
controversy. . . . I'm hoping there will be a vigorous
controversy . . . whether people end by taking my
suggestions or not . . . the most important objective
in my book would be to have a vigorous national debate
among educators and laymen on the question of how to
educate the teachers of American youth." [2] This volume is a testimony to Conant's success in that regard
and especially to his effectiveness in reaching and arous-
ing professional educators.

This book has been pursued in the belief that an
examination of the dispute in calm retrospect will contribute to increased understanding of the issues and of
their relevance to the future direction of teacher education in the United States. It became apparent during
the height of the political and intellectual skirmishes
about *The Education* that communication between
persons with contrasting opinions in American education has been exceedingly limited and was long overdue.
The controversy was marked by strong differences of
opinion by those committed to opposing conceptions,
but neither two-way dialogue nor two-way debate developed. Ideas were expressed unilaterally, with little or no
exploration of the differences. Political factions formed;
verbal attacks and defenses prevailed. Genuine conversation is still needed among those with radically opposed notions about how best to educate American
teachers.

As Conant has written, "A logical and a rational
view of education should logically be a product of one's
social philosophy." [3] There is a need to understand Conant's teacher education positions in the perspective of
both his socioeducational philosophy and his life. Some
of the statements of those who reacted to *The Educa-*

tion evidenced a lack of knowledge about Conant and his socioeducational philosophy. This is partly because of his tendency to resist personal publicity. He prefers the focus to be on what he considers more consequential—the subjects on which he writes. Despite his outstanding and varied career, which led in July of 1963 to his being awarded the Presidential Medal of Freedom, there is to date not even a single-volume biography of Conant. A multivolume biography of Conant is being prepared under the direction of Merle Borrowman (see the Preface), with the understanding that it will only be published after Conant, who is in his mid-seventies, dies.

Conant is preparing an autobiography, but there has still not been a definitive study or analysis of him or of his socioeducational outlook. In 1968, James E. McClellan of Temple University published, as chapter two of *Toward an Effective Critique of American Education,* the most complete and perceptive logical analysis in print of Conant's education orientation.[4] Conant's positions are rooted in contemporary American thought. This may help explain both his popularity and the previous lack of a solidly critical appraisal of his positions. Dominant views receive heavier criticism during their period of emergence and decline than during their prevalency. This writer hopes this first chapter will contribute to an understanding of Conant's teacher education positions in relationship to his socioeducational philosophy and life. In the concluding chapter, I try to compare and assess Conant's views with the other possible outlooks depicted and constructed in this book.

Some 5,000 complimentary paperback copies of *The Education* were mailed in envelopes bearing the "Conant Report" label to chief state school officers, deans of

schools of education, selected city superintendents, and
other key education officials about a week prior to the
release of the regular hardcover edition. *The Education*
was the second of his studies termed the "Conant Report"; *The American High School Today* (1959) also
contained specific proposals and was labeled "The Conant Report." Because of his many significant accomplishments and positions, the Conant name has stature
as well as status. The reports were part of his "A Study
of American Education" project, sponsored by a six-
year grant of almost a million dollars from the Carnegie
Corporation of New York. The total project, including
the reports, was administered for him by the Educational Testing Service of Princeton, New Jersey.

The Education was based on a two-year exploration
of conditions in seventy-seven teacher-training institutions in twenty-two states and of certification policies in
the sixteen most populous states, which contain two-
thirds of the population of the United States. *The Education* was the most extensive examination of American
teacher education since the U.S. Office of Education
published its *National Survey* thirty years earlier and
the American Council on Education conducted its
study between 1938 and 1944. Conant's thorough investigation of prevailing arrangements and practices as-
sured that *The Education* would not be ignored by educators, despite the strong criticisms that it contained.

The education *of* teachers has existed in some form
as long as teaching has been an occupation. Schooling
especially to prepare individuals *for* teaching is relatively new. By the title of his book as well as its content,
Conant evidenced his leaning to the older, broader, traditional view which originally stressed general education
and, only in the 19th century, added professional

teacher-education to university curricula. The technical portion had previously been part of schooling in what were initially institutions of reform, such as normal schools and teachers' seminaries, and in colleges and institutes rather than in the universities. Because many struggles were necessary to establish the professional education of teachers at college or university level, teacher education has become more identified with that phase than with the general or liberal aspects. At the same time, professional preparation has not commanded the respect and acceptance accorded liberal education.

Defining teacher education as only the technical aspect has lowered the standing of teacher education just as the absence of professional education studies in universities has reflected and abetted the low status of teaching. Because of the nature of teaching functions, the education of the person who is going to teach cannot be viewed as totally unrelated to the preparation of the individual for teaching. Many academicians believe that general education should be constructed separately from one's professional or vocational pursuits in order to be called a liberal education. A general or a professional course or program is liberal to the degree to which it actually assists people to be themselves and to develop to their fullest potential, whether vocational aims are involved or not. Work is a significant part of most people's lives. A liberal education adequate to the modern world, in contrast to ancient Athens where being a citizen was a vocation, seems to require some concern with one's occupational choice and role.

Conant does not seem to fall easily into a particular ideological camp. He is generally a realist, drawing philosophically upon the traditions of both rationalism and empiricism. Scientist Conant's contributions to education are embedded in what appear, at first glance, simply as attempts to apply the sense-realist empirical approach. That tradition may be traced back to Aristotle and others in ancient Greece, but it began to re-emerge in the modern world in the humanistic or verbal realism of Juan Luis Vives (1492–1540). Vives emphasized knowledge in relation to use, tangible and concrete measurable data, the everyday practical world of things in addition to the merely literary and verbal, use of the vernacular in schools as well as the classical tongues, and educating for character development. Michel de Montaigne (1533–1592) developed this further into what has since been termed "social realism" by adding a concern for providing upper-class youth with the proper social experiences to prepare them for success in life and career.

One of the first sense-realists was Richard Mulcaster (1530–1611), headmaster of two famous London academies, Merchant Taylor's and St. Paul's. Francis Bacon (1561–1626) and Johann Amos Comenius (1592–1670) were both indebted to Mulcaster. He not only stressed the use of the senses in learning but also, like Conant, a more empirical-inductive approach to teaching, and university involvement in teacher education. In *Positions* (1582), Mulcaster sought a graduate college of education:

There will be some difficulty in winning a college for those who will afterwards pass to teach in the schools. There is no specializing for any profession till the student leaves the College of Philosophy, from which he will go to Medicine, Law, or Divinity. This is the time also when the intending schoolmaster should begin his special training. In him there is as much learning necessary as, with all deference to their subjects, is required by any of the other three professions, especially if it be considered how much the teacher hath to do in preparing scholars for all other careers. Why should not these men have this competence in learning? . . . Why should not teachers be well provided for, so that they can continue their whole life in the schools, as divines, lawyers, and physicians do in their several professions? If this were the case, judgment, knowledge, and discretion would grow in them as they get older, whereas now the school, being used but for a shift, from which they will afterwards pass to some other profession, though it may send out competent men to other careers, remains itself far too bare of talent, considering the importance of the work. I consider therefore that in our universities there should be a special college for the training of teachers, inasmuch as they are the instruments to make or mar the growing generation of the country, and because the material of their studies is comparable to that of the greatest professions where in the forming of the mind and the exercising of the body require the most careful consideration, to say nothing of the dignity of character which should be expected from them.[5]

It was not until 1810, in Germany, that universities actually became directly involved in more than the general education of teachers. Johann Friedrich Herbart's pedagogical seminar was then officially recognized at the University of Konigsburg where he held the chair in philosophy previously occupied by Immanuel Kant. It was nearly the beginning of the twentieth century when university graduate schools of education began to develop, with the first being at New York University and Teachers College, Columbia University.

Throughout most of history, teaching has been learned directly on the job by unsupervised trial and error experience methods. Most professors in colleges and universities still learn to teach primarily by doing.

Their only requirement remains knowledge of the subject matter in the field to be taught. It is difficult for some professors to understand why any requirements in addition to a liberal education or subject-matter specialization are necessary for teachers at the elementary and secondary school levels. Proposals that college teachers receive some professional preparation for their teaching responsibilities in higher education are often met with disdain by academic professors. There has been some receptivity to the idea of professional preparation for the junior college level where teaching is recognized as a main concern and does not conflict with research goals.

Majors are growing in the field of higher education for those who seek college administrative posts, and organizations like the American Council on Education are trying experimental institutes to supplement the background of professors who go into administration. In the beginning of *The Education*, Conant admits to having been suspicious of any professional education courses while he was a member of Harvard's chemistry faculty and until he assumed Harvard's presidency in 1933. Like many university administrators, he then had to face the problems of how much general education, subject matter concentration, and professional preparation should go into the education of teachers and in what proportion and relationship.

Teaching has historically been a second-class occupation. Apprenticeship persisted in colonial America as the main route by which elementary schoolkeepers were prepared. For centuries, universities provided the general education and academic specialization for those who were to join their own faculties. Those who failed at that or at such other high professional goals as law, politics, medicine, or the ministry might then seek employment as teachers in the secondary classical Latin grammar schools or academies. Only recently has the gap in status almost entirely abated between the previously somewhat university-educated secondary teacher and the formerly nonuniversity trained elementary one. However, differences remain between preparing for teaching at the elementary and secondary levels. At many colleges, the education professors advise those anticipating elementary and junior high teaching, while academic professors advise those entering senior high teaching. More cooperation between academicians and educationists is needed at both levels.

A substantial number of elementary-school teachers still come from state colleges (former normal schools and teachers colleges), which, despite recent development into multipurpose institutions, usually have less status, heavier teaching and advisory loads, and lower academic and financial student prerequisites than most graduate university centers. Most state planning continues to support the university's hierarchical position in higher education, as does Conant who also seeks more university involvement in teacher education. The prestige of an occupation or an institution lies in the quality of individuals it can attract and the degree of selectivity it can employ. These factors affect finances and the quality and amount of preparation for teaching that can be anticipated or required. Still it should be added, state colleges remain more heavily involved in teacher education and are more especially concerned with teaching and the actual performance of their product than some of the more prestigious institutions with more diverse functions. However, current efforts in many states, such as New Jersey and New York, are to understress teacher education in favor of building the "arts and sciences." While this frequently masquerades as "liberal education," it is most often nothing more than "arts and sciences" professionalism.

When indentured servants worked off their bondage by apprenticing for teaching, conditions were so poor that many apprentices ran away. Institutions of higher learning in those times could not have been expected to assume responsibility for preparing people for such jobs. The trustees of Benjamin Franklin's 1750 Philadelphia academy were first to suggest that educating elementary teachers be a secondary-school aim. They declared:

. . . a number of the poorer Sort will be hereby qualified to act as Schoolmasters in the Country, to teach Children Reading, Writing, Arithmetic, and the Grammar of their Mother Tongue, and being of good morals and known character, may be recommended from the Academy to country Schools for that purpose; the Country suffering at present very much for want of good Schoolmasters, and obliged frequently to employ in their Schools, vicious imported Servants, or concealed Papists, who by their bad Examples and Instructions often deprave the Morals or corrupt the Principles of the Children under their care.[6]

Reflected is both eighteenth-century nativism and an acceptance of the fact that schoolteaching was mainly for "the poorer Sort."

The early nineteenth-century debates about whether elementary teachers should be educated in the academies or in the normal schools of the United States had three underlying issues: how much stress should be placed on general education and how much on professional training; whether teachers should be prepared in a university or nonuniversity track; whether their preparation should be in multipurpose or singlepurpose institutions. The last two issues are less consequential since normal schools became teachers colleges and now these are developing into multipurpose state colleges and even universities. As Merle Borrowman noted in 1965: "My estimate, based on reports gathered for James Bryant Conant's *The Education of American Teachers* . . . is that approximately 90 percent of the teachers were trained in 'multipurpose' institutions preparing more than one hundred teachers per year. The data was not reproduced in this form in the Conant volume." [7] Borrowman also pointed out that while singlepurpose institutions encouraged the craft approach, they also fostered teaching as a calling by involving academic faculty in that unitary goal.

Normal schools began as a separate track from the academy-university and thus initially prevented the expansion of higher education. One of the ironies in the history of American education is that they eventually provided relatively inexpensive and increased opportunities for college and graduate work. Conant has favored the multipurpose aspect, while having been quite cautious in the past about the expansion of advanced university study. He urges on the part of the total university the dedication to teacher education that has primarily characterized the singlepurpose institutions and the separatist university schools of education which he opposes.

When conducted properly, apprenticeship teacher education had the advantage of providing some kind of supervised induction not otherwise available. But since apprenticeship was associated with lower-class occupations, it had the disadvantage of maintaining the inferior status of teaching. Conant heavily stresses the clinical experience of teachers. It was the one professional component of the report on which he states that he found almost total agreement. The clinical professorship fits Conant's realist bent. Another reason for this emphasis may be because university faculties have traditionally disavowed job-training as a main function, even though they directly service their own professions and others. While science faculties produce scientists and social science departments, social scientists, the traditional liberal ideal has been Platonic in upholding the primacy of theoretical considerations over practical or applied vocational ones. In his *Anti–Intellectualism in American Life* (1963) Richard Hofstadter defined intellectualism as concern with knowledge apart from its use. Conant shares that purist intellectual concept but he also advocates university training for the professions. He wants those aspiring to positions of societal leadership to receive a liberal education of the sort he advocated at Harvard in the forties.

Robert Maynard Hutchins has decried professionalism as being akin to both vocationalism and materialistic commercialism in detracting from the liberal intellectual aims of higher education in the pursuit of pure truth. Arthur E. Bestor Jr. and James D. Koerner, among others, have made more specific claims that professional education courses detract from academic ones. Clark Kerr's "multiversity" construct allows for all kinds of functions, relationships, balance or the lack of it between the liberal and technical aspects of higher education. Unlike the academic purism of Hutchins, Bestor, and Koerner, and the laissez-faire pluralism of Kerr, Conant has asserted:

The cultivation of learning alone produces not a university but a research institute; sole concern with student life produces in these days either an academic country club or a football team maneuvering under a collegiate banner; professional education by itself results in nothing but a trade school; an institution concerned with general education, even in the best liberal arts tradition, divorced from research and training for the professions is admittedly not a university but a college. Therefore, to my mind, the future of the American university depends primarily on keeping a balance between these four traditional elements of strength.[8]

Because many professional educationists are sensitive to the way in which apprenticeship helped maintain teaching's nonprofessional status, some construed Conant's strong emphasis on clinical experience to mean that he conceived of education more as a craft or a trade than as a profession. His limitation of the amount of schooling considered desirable prior to teaching was another reason why some believed Conant reduced teaching to a craft or trade status. Conant was also criticized for failing to require either a specific theoretical basis for teaching or any graduate work before one begins to teach. In 1950, Conant stated that "specialized training, be it at a professional or a vocational level, is best obtained right on the job. To be sure, the teaching of certain skills and the imparting of specialized knowledge must be included in many programs." [9] What many educationists did not realize was that Conant, as he later explained, assumed the understanding of his definition of a profession as a job requiring university preparation. He was therefore not explicit enough on this point in his advocacy of an "all-university" approach to teacher education. Conant has tended to link the attainment of a complete professional standing for teaching with a more widespread acceptance of the "all-university" approach. He not only wants the academic man more involved, but also teachers exposed to a university research atmosphere. One contemporary problem is that such institutions, especially the private ones, if they reward effective teaching at all, do so only after grantsmanship, publishing, and research.

From early times, schooling has been used to maintain and gain social position, to promote social stability and social fluidity. Apart from the political-religious leaders who taught, the first teachers were scribes whose vocational tools of reading, writing and reckoning earned them positions of eminence. For reasons of job protection, they did not desire their skills to become common knowledge. The first Athenian elementary schools were private and only available to those children of the free citizenry who could afford them. In contrast, Plato believed the selection process should be based on the talent and ability of the child, not on the wealth or social position of the parents. His "operation headstart" was for all children. He proposed state boarding nursery schools with student uniforms to eliminate social class distinctions.

The word "school" comes from the Greek *schole* meaning leisure. A surplus economy rather than a subsistence one has generally been necessary to afford the time for instruction. As a rule, the more personal and societal luxury, the more schooling that can be provided and utilized. The more advanced levels of schooling have historically been for the upper-status groups. The lower elementary schools have frequently been objects of disdain for the elite who preferred instead to use private tutors for their children or to teach them themselves. Lawrence A. Cremin, Henry Barnard Professor of Education at Teachers College, Columbia University, explains in *The American Common School* (1951), that even by the nineteenth century, when the common or elementary public schools were developing in the United States, it had to be stated plainly that they were to be common to all, not merely for commoners.

Teacher status has been tied to the levels of schooling both achieved and taught, especially as these have been related to the social-class background of both pupil and teacher. Attempts to increase the schooling of teachers beyond the grades they teach have been efforts to raise the social and professional standing of teaching. The amount of schooling necessary to teach at a particular level remains mainly a function of the level to be taught. The more selective, "higher" grades have had both greater prerequisites and greater prestige than the "lower," "secondary," and "elementary" ones. Even today, these "lower" grades are associated with masses of poor children, inconsequential play, rudimentary learning, and women. While there is a growing awareness of the vital importance of the early grades, they still lack in esteem in contrast to the higher pursuit of truth by an aristocracy of male adult leaders preparing for serious professional endeavors. The ancient Roman elementary school was called *ludi*, meaning "to play," probably indicating both the leisure it required and its subordinate status. In Thailand today, a teacher with a master's degree is required to teach at the secondary rather than the elementary level. Compulsory school laws, the abolition of child labor, and the growth of child psychology have helped to reduce but not to eliminate this aristocratic heritage in the United States. The concern with public schooling of such an illustrious person as former

Harvard president Conant has also contributed to its esteem, despite his "high" administrative perspective.

The association of teacher education with the "lower" elementary and secondary levels of schooling delayed its assimilation into "higher" education as did the inferior status of teaching in general. In 1903 George Bernard Shaw wrote in *Man and Superman*, "He who can, does. He who cannot, teaches." To this has been added that those who cannot teach, teach teachers; and even that those who cannot do that, become administrators. The first attack helps keep teacher salaries low; the teachers then scapegoat administrators whose pay differential is high. The newness of teacher training and of pedagogy in higher education also was a factor in maintaining their low standing in comparison with other university endeavors. In 1939, Conant recognized that "the so-called 'social sciences,' which include education are in their infancy." [10] In 1969 the growth of public governmental and private foundational support of education has increased concern with professional education in colleges and universities, but the study of education has yet to be recognized as worthy of academic and liberal concentration for persons who do not choose teaching as their vocation. Agencies, outlooks, and systems in politics and economics are studied as a part of general education, but such an examination of education remains neglected. For a long time the academic man has scapegoated the field of education to enhance his own professionalism.

Over the years, Conant has upheld the selective nature of university education. In 1938 he wrote, "University education for all is to me a contradiction in terms." [11] He has opposed the word "higher" in higher education not merely because of the prestige factor, but

also b   ieves that it lures many far beyond
their   this, he is both Platonic and Jeffersonian   n is Conant's educational idol). The re-
cen   loped federal antipoverty education pro-
gr   o assume both inherent ability and variation
a   individuals. They seek to equalize the talent race
by compensating for differential environmental support
of the socially-desired and school-rewarded talents.

Also like Plato and Jefferson, Conant believes that
schools must provide complete equality of opportunity
by sorting persons by individual ability rather than by
family wealth or social station. One of Conant's first
endeavors as Harvard's president was to seek national
scholars, and later national merit scholarships, because
"we should be able to say that any man with remarkable
talents may obtain his education at Harvard, whether
he be rich or penniless, whether he come from Boston
or San Francisco. . . . The universities in this country
should be the apex of a pyramid based on our highly
developed school system. A path to the top should be
open to all of exceptional talent. The privately endowed
institutions must keep the way clear for the gifted
youth with limited means." [12] Those who criticized Conant for his long association with a highly-selective
Eastern private university demonstrated their ignorance
of how he had worked to transform its socially aristocratic aspects, though not its intellectual ones. Conant
has tended to ignore the possibility that the latter cannot be separated from the former because of the impact
of social class on the socialization process and because
of class-biased measures of intelligence.

President Roosevelt ordered the banks closed only a
few months before Conant was inaugurated as Harvard's top administrator. The lengthiest published ac-

count of Conant's life states: "The Harvard Corporation picked Conant for president of the university very strongly for the reason that members felt he gave the best promise of bringing the university through the depression by introducing economies to produce a balanced budget." [13] Conant has himself indicated that he opposes waste, but he does not think of that as "frugality" or "timidness" regarding spending.[14] Despite the depression, he seems to have had to contain the annual budget only once in his twenty years as Harvard's chief administrator, and never to have reduced it. He is also known for his personnel policy whereby junior department members would know exactly how many and when senior tenure appointments would be made. They were then knowingly "up or out," as critics termed the procedure. Conant regards such free and open competition as both desirable and fair.

Charles W. Eliot, also a chemist by training and the only previous Harvard president Conant tends to refer to by name, had written in 1869, "It were a bitter mockery to suggest that any subject whatever should be taught less than it now is. . . . It will be generations before the best of American institutions will get growth enough to 'bear pruning . . .'" In 1936 Conant quoted the Eliot statement and then countered:

It is now sixty-seven years since this statement was made and three generations have passed; in my opinion the time for pruning has arrived. The faculties should endeavor to reduce the number of courses given and in many cases to condense the material now presented. The tremendous subdivision of the fields of learning which has occurred in the past thirty-five years will certainly shock the academic historian a century from now. And the increase in the number of special courses of instruction has by no means been solely in the Faculty of Arts and Sciences; the professional schools have shown the same tendency. How to stop this movement of expansion, how to eliminate and condense, how to arrive at an agreement on certain aspects of certain subjects which should be thoroughly mastered, - to my mind these are the great educational questions of the future.[15]

Chemist Conant became a university president in 1932—not only during the depression but also during Hitler's rise to power in Germany. These events were to affect deeply Conant's life and philosophy as they did so many others. Conant's first direct study of education had been an eight-month visit in 1925 to investigate research and teaching methods in the German universities. While he never wrote formally about that trip, he has spoken of it positively on many occasions. In 1958, five years after Conant had resigned from Harvard's stewardship to accept appointment by President Eisenhower as U.S. Commissioner to West Germany and later Ambassador to the Federal Republic of Germany, Conant recalled: "Those of my generation who studied in German universities in the 1920s could not fail to be impressed both by the quantity and calibre of the scientific work and by the recognition accorded to scholars and scientists by people in all walks of life. Judged from the standpoint of a university teacher, German education in the Weimar Republic seemed excellent indeed. Then came Hitler and his gangsters, the rape of the universities. . . ."[16] In a 1964 "Credo," Conant wrote of that 1925 visit: "While I was then a chemist talking to other chemists, the differences between the organization of instruction and research in American and German universities made a profound impression on me and to a degree influenced my attitude later as President of Harvard." [17]

Conant's emphasis on the social responsibilities of universities and their faculties seems related to his distress over the Nazi impact on the German universities. In *Abuse of Learning* (1948), Frederick Lilge maintained that German professors were diverted from societal concerns by research grants on very specialized socially irrelevant topics. The professors were bought and indirectly became tools of the dominant power forces. Like many of the American educators who visited the pre-Nazi German universities before him, Conant developed a strong admiration for their spirit of free inquiry, promotion of professional graduate studies, and support of research despite the lingering effects of inflation. In 1950, Conant stated:

It has been fashionable in recent years, after the holocaust of two world wars, to decry the importation to this continent of the spirit of the German university. It has likewise been easy to put all the blame for what happened in Germany on the German universities as they developed in the nineteenth century. On the theory of *post hoc ergo propter hoc*, of course this assignment of guilt can be readily undertaken. One might venture to suggest, however, that there were a few other variable factors, and I for one am a quite unrepentant enthusiast for what the German universities did for the advance of civilization between the Napoleonic War and the end of the nineteenth century. Therefore, to my mind, much of the spirit of those institutions as centers for advancing knowledge and training of future professors in the arts and letters still is a valuable inheritance in the American past. On the whole I should say that this inheritance has been whittled away by events in this century and we are in danger of neglecting it rather than of overemphasizing it. In saying this I rec-

ognize that I am betraying my prejudices based on my long
career as a research man myself.[18]

The new stress in universities and colleges on securing
funds from government and from private foundations
accompanies also the adoption in the United States of
the German university research model.

Conant questioned the thesis that the German universities had been a main factor in the Nazi ascent to
power. In his 1958 Godkin Lectures, Conant expressed
dubiousness about the thesis of an English writer who
in 1916 blamed the First World War on the German
academic stimulus causing healthy ambition to become
"morbid." Conant also acknowledged the dangers to
which I am alluding when he suggested in 1958 that
"Germany of the Nazi period" made:

. . . the most ardent believer in education . . . realize
how carefully he must formulate his creed. Qualifications
are in order that were undreamed of when this century
was young. An excellent system of education (or what appears to be an excellent system) does not automatically
guarantee freedom. On the contrary, it may be one element
in a national system that is but the prelude to a loss of
freedom. This is one of the lessons of the rise of Hitler, the
one most relevant to those concerned with schools and universities.

The Nazi period itself provides another lesson. Certain
types of excellent education, or at least excellent types of
advanced training in certain professions, may go hand in
hand with a suppression of freedom.[19]

He concluded:

. . . on the note on which I ventured to begin—the significance for Germany, past, present, and future, of educa-

tion, and the writings of the learned man. The schools and universities of Germany have been blamed (perhaps unduly) for much that has happened in the past. For the next period, they will be potent influences in determining the way educated Germans think about the past and envision the future of their land.[20]

Conant's emphasis on selectivity in university education related to his view of what had happened in Germany. For his statement about graduate schools in his 1936–1937 President's Report that "no one knows how serious is the unemployment of university men, but it seems to me highly probable that a diminution in the total number of students in the universities of this country is desirable," he came under assault from the Cambridge Union of University Teachers, an American Federation of Teachers affiliate organized in the fall of 1935.[21] When seeking scholarships for the talented poor, Conant indicated consistently that he did not desire to enlarge university enrollments. By 1938, he made the connection with Germany explicit:

I am inclined to think that probably there are too many rather than too few students attending the universities of the country. I should very much question the desirability of increasing materially the number in our professional schools. Indeed, in some instances the number might well be reduced. The social problems created by serious unemployment in the professions are obvious. The German experience in the decade after the War should warn us against the perils lying in wait for a nation which trains a greater number of professional men than society can employ.[22]

In addition to his Jeffersonianism, Conant feared the disruptive effects on a free society of a frustrated, unemployed professional class. He had urged the limiting of enrollments because he anticipated a stable population by 1960. His reluctance to stress teaching as a profession may be linked to these earlier fears as well as to his acute awareness of the field's shortcomings.

Conant has not been opposed to increasing the number of people having some kind of post-secondary education. In the 1938 article, he also expressed his preference for the selective non-local university type of four-year liberal arts college, but he added that a two-year junior college course might be desirable for almost every youth. Ten years later, and again in 1956, he advocated that about half of the appropriate age group could benefit from a terminal two-year junior college program. He defended such expansion on the grounds that it would not cause an abundance of unemployed professionals such as could occur with an increase in the enrollments of four-year colleges which readily lead on to graduate study. He asserted that junior colleges should not be looked down upon as inferior institutions for the rejects of other colleges. Neither should they siphon off those especially talented youth who ought to attend four-year university-type colleges.

Conant disliked the "junior" label for implying a transfer function to "senior" institutions. He therefore recommended that the two-year community college grant a Bachelor of General Studies degree. In 1966, he repeated this suggestion, but advocated that all high school graduates who want more education should continue in either a junior or a four-year college. By then he seems to have accepted the transfer as well as the terminal junior college function.[23] His concerns regarding an unemployed professional class may have markedly diminished. He may have revised his thinking and have accepted the junior college transfer function as desirable. Since he still favored a terminal degree for the junior college, he may have merely decided that the transfer function was a politically unalterable practice, even though still undesirable. In "Closing the Gap," a January 28, 1968 article on the education page of *The New York Times* "News of the Week" section, M. A. Farber reported that Conant was still asserting the need to emphasize the two-year community college and to deemphasize the four-year prestige Bachelor of Arts degree course and college.

In his 1952 dissertation on "James Bryant Conant's Conceptions of the Structuring of Educational Functions," James E. Perdue, president of the State University of New York at Oswego, suggested that Conant had failed to connect adequately the general educational functions and the investigational research ones and thus had not addressed himself sufficiently to university college adult education or the four-year nonuniversity unitary liberal arts colleges where those purposes most conflict. Conant's stress on university teacher preparation does not fully account for the fact that most universities presently reward grant-getting and research much more than good teaching. While he has occasionally decried that situation, his own strong commitment to a research orientation seems dominant.

Conant has been called a conservative, a moderate, a liberal in quotes, and even both a collectivist and a fascist. He has referred to himself as an American radical and an educational Calvinist. Which terms apply depend upon what aspects of his social and educational philosophy are being alluded to and from what frame of reference. Conservative, elitist, and aristocratic have been used by Jacksonians who desire the expansion of higher education without Conant's emphasis on selectivity. Those adjectives also come from liberal educators who dislike Conant's allegiances to the gifted, to the traditional school aims of transmitting subject matter and to maintaining America's basic social patterns. Speaking in 1960 on "The Relevance of Jefferson's Ideas Today," Conant conceded: "To advocate a selective system of free higher education was to be accused of being undemocratic." [24]

In 1964, Conant spoke of himself as a "proponent of revolutionary change in practice teaching and its supervision." [25] In 1965 Merle Borrowman wrote:

In the present era, one in which *The Education of American Teachers* by the conservative James Bryant Conant has rocked the education establishment with charges that it is excessively rigid, overly committed to standardization, and not as imaginative as it could be, one is fascinated to read the same criticisms leveled a generation ago by men on the democratic left. The Social Frontiersmen were temperamentally rebellious; Conant is not. Can it be that the tendencies that blocked the aspirations of radicals thirty years ago have become so exaggerated that now even the moderate is frustrated? [26]

In criticizing *The Education*, Robert H. Beck, professor of history and philosophy of education at the University of Minnesota, called Conant a "liberal" but only in contrast to the earlier, more "conservative" Albert Jay Nock who had also stressed Jeffersonianism.[27] Conant is more liberal than those Jeffersonians like Nock or Norman Foerster or Gustave Mueller who have emphasized selectivity without also stressing equality of opportunity. Jacksonians interpret Conant as less liberal than they because he does not urge the expan-

sion of educational opportunity independent of a selecting and sorting process. They view Jefferson as essentially a Jacksonian who stressed selectivity only to make
his 1779 "Bill for the More General Diffusion of
Knowledge" in Virginia appear more politically acceptable to the conservatives; it was still considered too radical and failed to secure legislative approval. Conant's
emphasis on selectivity may be more realistic than the
Jacksonian neglect of it, but as Thomas Green, professor of education at Syracuse University, has pointed out
to me, stress on selectivity can lead to an emphasis on
the sorting and certifying aspects of schools rather than
on their teaching and guidance functions.

Both Jacksonians and Jeffersonians seem to agree
that selectivity on the wrong bases does already occur.
One question before American society is whether the
aim ought to be to eliminate all educational selectivity,
except as related to occupational and professional
preparation, or only the wrong kinds of selectivity in
general and liberal schooling. The problem of which of
these goals to call the "liberal position" points up the
inherent difficulties of such terms, as does the diversity
of labels which have been applied to Conant's views.
But as R. Freeman Butts developed in *The College
Charts Its Course* (1939) and Roy E. Lieuallen showed
in his dissertation, "The Jeffersonian and Jacksonian
Conceptions in Higher Education" (1954), Jeffersonians like Conant stress selectivity, standards, and tracking, while Jacksonians emphasize increased length and
higher quality of schooling for expanded numbers. The
issue is the meaning of equal educational opportunity.

By calling himself an "American radical" in 1943,
Conant meant that, as contrasted with European radicals, he favored free enterprise, free competition, and

the profit system of rewards; but as opposed to American reactionaries, he sought a society without hereditary classes:

No one needs to be told that the American radical will be a fanatic believer in equality. Yet it will be a peculiar North American brand of doctrine. For example, he will be quite willing in times of peace to let net salaries and earnings sail way above the $25,000 mark. He believes in equality of opportunity, not equality of rewards; but on the other hand, he will be lusty in wielding the axe against the root of inherited privilege. To prevent the growth of a caste system, which he abhors, he will be resolute in his demand to confiscate (by constitutional methods) all property once a generation. He will demand really effective inheritance and gift taxes and the breaking up of trust funds and estates. And this point cannot be lightly pushed aside, for it is the kernel of his radical philosophy.[28]

For his statement about confiscating property, Conant was called a collectivist by Alexander Lincoln, a Harvard alumnus who was sufficiently disturbed with Conant's greater egalitarianism and liberalism to privately print his own diatribe against Conant.[29] It is quite clear from all of Conant's writings that he could only have been so labeled by what Conant dubbed an American reactionary or by one totally oblivious to Conant's other positions, even those expressed in the same article. Lincoln had also been irked in 1935 by Harvard's awarding an honorary degree to the late Henry A. Wallace, then Secretary of Agriculture. A 1953 *Catholic World* article by M. Whitcomb Hess decried "Conant's Big Business Fascism" and lamented that the "working out of the Conant Unholy Alliance of democracy-business is education's task." [30] Hess lambasted Conant not only for advocating a secular unified society stressing competition, private enterprise and the profit motive but also for his defense and support of public education as the means of strengthening that culture. The use of the terms "collectivist" and "fascist" by the extreme critics of Conant demonstrates their ignorance of his devotion to a free society; Hess, however, was aware that Conant meant a free enterprise economic system.

To support his complaint that Conant's views were not based on a set of religious principles, Hess relied heavily on an earlier pamphlet by Oliver Martin, a philosophy professor. Martin also criticized Conant's cooperation with business and industry, his nonmetaphysical orientation, and the 1945 Harvard Report on *General Education in a Free Society* (which Conant both initiated and endorsed) for not specifically recommending that a course in philosophy be a college graduation requirement. Martin bemoaned that loss by terming it a "tragedy" that Conant "should elevate moral nihilism and anti-intellectualism into a principle." [31] If one defines intellectualism traditionally as a concern with knowledge totally independent of its social consequences or use (as do Hofstadter and did Martin), one might consider Conant an intellectual in some ways and an anti-intellectual in others. He accepts a purist conception for the liberal arts and sciences and favors an operational construct in subjects he considers applied. He values both approaches and both kinds of learning but he conceives of them as belonging to distinct and separate spheres. As a realist, Conant accepts the existing conceptual and institutional contexts, and operates within them. In *The Education*, he was concerned with the applied professional preparation of teachers rather than with the study of the field of education as a social science. He thus discussed the latter only in terms of the former.

To return to Conant's 1943 *Atlantic Monthly* defense of the "American radical": The radical is valuable not merely because "he favors public education, truly universal educational opportunity at every level" and "would bemoan the cynicism of our youth and the intellectual dishonesty of our age and might well be fanatical in his desire for certain reforms in education," but also because he is aware of "the dangers of Federal control of institutions concerned with youth" and realizes that the "only hope of preventing his hereditary enemy, the Federal power, from increasing every decade is to strengthen local government." [32] Conant acknowledged that government had to play a larger role in an industrial than in an agrarian society, but in contrast to "European radicals," Conant stood for decentralization and local responsibility. Although Conant supported Democrat Al Smith in 1928, he was at one time listed in *Who's Who* as a Republican; his political affiliation was later omitted. He has held federal appointments during both Democratic and Republican administrations; the first was more related to his scientific competencies; the second, to his political.

Conant's distrust of federalism showed itself in his 1964 book *Shaping Educational Policy*. Conant proposed that a nationwide policy in education should result from an interstate compact. Under the initial leadership of Terry Sanford, when he was governor of North Carolina, that proposal has materialized, but two different articles in the same issue of one newspaper criticized the compact, on the one hand, for being too

separate from the existing federal agencies and on the
other, for going too far, too fast, in the direction of state
centralization.[33]

Despite the political implementation of the compact, *Shaping Educational Policy* received less attention
than *The Education* but came under more severe criticism. Richard Wynn, associate dean of the School of
Education at the University of Pittsburgh, termed
Shaping "An Inept Lesson in Educational Policy Making," and Paul Nash, professor of education at Boston
University, in his review of *Shaping* lamented of Conant: "His position and influence are enormous. His
views are listened to and followed. It is all the more sad,
therefore, and may even turn out to be tragic, that, at
this vital juncture in the history of American education
its chief spokesman should be a man of such conservative instincts, such limited vision, and such timid
imagination." [34]

In his 1966 article on "The Interstate Compact,"
Franklin Parker, Benedum Professor of Education at
West Virginia University, spoke of the compact as be-
ing a result of a "new guard" in education. Parker iden-
tified this group as including, in addition to Conant,
John W. Gardner (identified in the first paragraph of
this chapter), Terry Sanford (mentioned earlier),
Francis Keppel (appointed by Conant as dean of
Harvard's Graduate School of Education, by President
Kennedy as U.S. Commissioner of Education, and
by President Johnson as Assistant U.S. Secretary of
Health, Education, and Welfare under Gardner [Kep-
pel's father had also been president of the Carnegie
Corporation before Gardner]), and Harold Howe II
(U.S. Commissioner of Education after Keppel; an ad-
ministrator at the Newton, Massachusetts public

schools, which received Carnegie Corporation funding of a team-teaching project developed in conjunction with Harvard's Master of Arts in teaching programs when Keppel was dean; and director of the Institute of Learning, which Terry Sanford developed in North Carolina with Carnegie Corporation grants when he was governor). At the same time that the Carnegie Corporation of New York sponsored Conant's *Shaping*, it was sponsoring with the Ford Foundation Terry Sanford's 1964 research on "A Study of American States," which aimed at increasing the role of the state in education. Of this "new guard," Parker wrote:

These new men in positions of educational power are essentially academic intellectuals oriented to university and foundation ivory-tower thinking. They are concerned with change and have been successful in the past in effecting change. But they are far removed from classroom teaching and their assumptions about public school needs will undoubtedly undergo serious revision when they have to wrestle at the grass roots level with elementary and secondary school programs and with school boards. We have yet to see this conservative "new guard" of the 1960s equal the reforms of the liberal progressives of the 1930s, whose democratic influence they apparently despise.

Armed with federal funds, backed by political power, urged by foundation reform tendencies, inspired by the Great Society concept, and given their mandate by the awesome challenges of our time, the "new guard" means to renovate American education with what they term "innovative excellence." [35]

Conant's influence has also been especially marked in New York State through James E. Allen, Jr., the State Education Commissioner who recently accepted the post of United States Commissioner of Education in President Nixon's administration.

Conant has considered student ability a greater determining factor in the educational process than teaching effectiveness. In 1937 he said, "I am, I must admit, an educational Calvinist. I have but little faith in salvation by good works and a large measure of belief in predestination if not at birth at least at the college entrance age." In the same talk, he expressed his reservations about too easily introducing new courses or fields: "I am not the hotel detective, but if I were, I should keep a sharp watch on certain of the most recent newcomers for they wear the flashy clothes of highly suspicious characters." [36] In his book *The Revolutionary Transformation of the American High School* (1959), Conant attributed that change from a selective to a mass institution to current employment conditions. In this situation, he felt the educators were merely responding rather than leading as they thought. In his earlier book, *Education in a Divided World* (1948), Conant expressed his belief that educationists have tended to think of themselves as social reformers who mistakenly believe they are farsighted. He believes constructive realists or hardheaded idealists are more effective than naive optimists in delineating and facing the social conditions of the times. Conant's realist bent probably also contributed to his interests in physical science and administration, and these areas tend to strengthen such a bias.

In depicting Conant strictly as an aristocratic elitist because of his concern with selectivity, the gifted, and early measurement of talent, Jacksonian educators tended to neglect his work as both a member and Chairman of the Educational Policies Commission (EPC) of the National Education Association (NEA).

Conant helped to develop and wholeheartedly supported the EPC's policy statement on *The Education of ALL American Youth* in 1944 and its 1951 sequel, *The Education of ALL American Youth: A Further Look*. Ten years later, Van Cleve Morris, then professor of philosophy of education at Rutgers University and currently at the Chicago campus of the University of Illinois, referred to these volumes as "perhaps the most explicit development of the Jacksonian thesis anywhere in educational literature." [37] Conant wants a differentiation of all acceptable talents as early as possible, but he has also warned that some cannot be measured too early. He speaks for artistic, physical, social, and practical talents as well as intellectual and "book-learning" ones. He relies heavily on testing procedures to identify these assets. It then becomes the function of guidance counselors to assist in the appropriate program planning. Such programs should foster the socially and personally constructive abilities of all youth, not merely the college bound.

Conant has chided both college professors for judging high schools strictly by their success with the academically gifted, and public school personnel for not being sufficiently concerned with the intellectually bright. Changes in those attitudes were the basic terms of a truce he proposed in 1945 between academicians and educationists. He favors secondary school ability grouping by subject, but in a single comprehensive institution to prevent "a segregation which might turn the boys and girls in question into either prigs or academic snobs." [38] He opposes small institutions which cannot provide sufficient facilities and personnel for extensive curriculum offerings and ability grouping. He values all socially useful occupations, but wants secondary schools and four-year colleges and universities to concentrate more on intellectual skills for the bright.

Because Conant's heavy involvement in studies of American education have brought him recently to the attention of the general school person, a number thought he was a newcomer to that area. Although his *Slums and Suburbs: A Commentary on Schools in Metropolitan Areas* was published in 1961, there was comment after *The Education* that Conant was just discovering the slums that have surrounded Harvard for years. Over twenty years earlier, in his "Education for a Classless Society: The Jeffersonian Tradition," Conant had asserted in reference to the lack of commuting colleges in non-urban areas: "In many localities the opportunities for the children of the really poor are lamentable indeed." [39] In his first presidents' report for 1933–1934, Conant was concerned about the area around Harvard, but in terms of living conditions to attract new faculty. In his recent *The Comprehensive High School* (1967), Conant included only three New York City Schools, telling Fred M. Hechinger, *The New York Times* education editor: "I did not want to deal with the problems of New York City. I don't understand New York. It shouldn't really exist." [40] Conant has shown his awareness of and concern for the inadequacies of both slum and rural schools but his knowledge of what such deprived environments really mean for those who dwell and subsist within them, seems to be mainly from a distant upper-middle class perspective.

As early as 1934, Conant spoke before the Middle States Association of Colleges and Secondary Schools on "The Function of the Secondary School and College in Educating for Social and Cultural Leadership." It was then that Conant first referred to himself as "a novice in education (with a capital E)," adding, "I am at a disadvantage in speaking before this association, and I cannot fall back on the stock-in-trade of my previous existence: lecture table experiments. I have no apparatus before me, no wine to change to water, no preparations for a scintillating combustion, no train laid for a startling explosion to wake you at the end, and I assure you I feel the lack of these auxiliaries most keenly." [41] His first book in 1920 was a secondary-school text, *Practical Chemistry*, co-authored with his former science master at the Roxbury Latin School.

Because of Conant's concern with selectivity and the gifted and his own marked professional success, many people have assumed that he himself never had any school problems. They then inferred that he was personally unable to speak adequately to the education of average and below-average youth. They also assumed that he was solely a private-school product. These assumptions are false. Conant began school in a public kindergarten in 1898 at the age of five and a half. There followed a couple of years of private schooling, after which he entered a Miss Baldam's third grade class in the Bailey Street Public School in his native Dorchester, Massachusetts. It was there that Bryant (as he was called to distinguish him from his father, James Scott Conant) was found to be a slow reader and poor writer, and received help in these subjects. Three years later when Bryant was applying to Roxbury Latin School, he initially failed the spelling portion of the admissions examination and came home in tears about it. He was fortunate to have outstanding scientific traits that were recognized, and to have been motivated and able to overcome his verbal weaknesses.

Conant was admitted to Roxbury Latin School at the age of eleven. Although he was editor of the school newspaper in his senior year, science was clearly Conant's forte. Several years before Bryant started at Roxbury, his father, a pioneer in the wood and photoengraving industry, had encouraged the scientific bent of his third child and only son. The father had built a lean-to laboratory for Bryant on the family house and given him a monthly allowance to purchase materials and equipment for his experiments. When selected by the Roxbury faculty to give an address at his 1910 commencement, Bryant chose instead to conduct a complex combustion explosion. With the exception of Conant's science master, the faculty was surprised at the skill of the demonstration and especially the adequacy of the youth's explanation. The Roxbury class seer predicted that Bryant would be a druggist "serving as a premium on all sales over three cents, a guaranteed chemically pure prussic acid ferrocyanide milkshake." [42] Little could that prophet have guessed that thirty-five years later Dr. Conant would be present at a New Mexico proving ground watching the mushroom cloud of an atomic explosion which he had a major part in coordinating and developing, or that his recent detonations would have been verbal ones in what historian Willis Rudy astutely dubbed "The 'Cold War' Among Educators." [43]

In June 1940, President Roosevelt appointed Conant a member of the National Defense Research Committee headed by Vannevar Bush. A year later, Conant became chairman of the committee. When Bush took over the Office of Scientific Research and Development, he appointed Conant deputy director in charge of overseeing atomic energy developments. During the First World War, Conant served as a Major in chemical warfare and helped develop the gas later called "Lewisite." As early as May of 1940, he had urged United States involvement to defeat Hitler; Conant has proudly recalled the refusal of the Harvard Board of Overseers to accept a donation from an intimate of Hitler despite the need for money during the first years of Conant's administration. Conant has long sought to preserve and to extend what he considers America's unique contribution to the world: "A demonstration that a certain type of society long dreamed of by idealists can be closely approached in reality—a free society in which the hopes and aspirations of a large part of the members find enduring satisfactions through outlets once reserved for only a small minority of mankind." [44]

One might speculate on how much of Conant's concern with the early identification and fostering of all acceptable abilities is related to the experiences of his own youth. In the 1930s he grouped collegiate talent into the literary-linguistic and the mathematical-scientific and he opposed college demands that youth with special talents of one sort must also be proficient in the other. Despite this opposition, he did favor some intellectually selective test:

I have tried to make it evident in what I have just said that I do not regard the requirements of high standing in old-fashioned subjects taken in large doses (concentration) as being the equivalent of training specialists. I consider such a procedure simply as being the only sure-fire selective machinery we possess. By the same token I refuse to admit that it is necessary to introduce special courses in order to provide training for citizenship or make available a liberal education. I believe in a well-balanced academic community with proper arrangements for social life among the students, the liberal element in education is largely supplied indirectly. Of course, this method is impossible where all or almost all of the students major in the same field whether it be applied science or the social sciences, or tap-dancing. Hence the need of having in every college of the liberal arts tradition, strong departments in all fields to attract able students. Hence the need of having a variety of subjects in which a student may major.[45]

Conant had been seeking to transform what was still essentially Harvard College into a strong, first-class graduate university, and he generally opposed sacrificing depth to breadth. He was against any specific course other than in a student's chosen major being required for college graduation. By 1945, he favored university distribution requirements with election among specific nonsurvey courses within broad areas of study, as recommended in the *General Education in a Free Society* report he helped sponsor. Van Cleve Morris has noted the "essentialist position" of that work; by essentialism he means that the prime concern is with transmitting content and skills considered basic and essential.[46] Conant's basic outlook had been that a liberal education came best in the informal social association of students in different fields such as occurred around the dining room tables in the Harvard house plan of living, initiated for post-freshmen by a 1930 grant from Edward Harkness. While he no longer favors such a totally voluntary approach, Conant once tried to institute among Harvard students an extracurricular study of American history such as he has personally pursued.

Conant's opposition to state-prescribed courses as the means of certifying teachers and his call for an interdisciplinary "all-university" approach necessitating a multipurpose rather than a single-purpose institution might be seen as logical extensions of his social conception of liberal education as well as of his belief in university autonomy. His stress on teacher education as a university rather than a college function appears to result in part from his general beliefs that teaching and research should accompany one another and that becoming a fully certified teacher ought to necessitate some graduate study. By promoting teacher education in a university setting, Conant hopes to attract the most intellectually able. This coincides with his advocacy of tracking at the college level by institution: the brightest at the colleges which are part of universities; the next group at the unitary nonuniversity four year college; and those of minimal college ability at the junior college.

This Platonic orientation is consciously in effect in California higher education, and is emerging in New York and New Jersey. It is generally implicit in the whole American higher educational scene and seems to reflect the social-class structure and the effective protection of their children's socioeconomic inheritance by upper-status families. While Conant explicitly opposes such favoritism, he generally neglects the positive correlation of school success with social class in his views on higher education. At the secondary level, he advocates the comprehensive high school with both heterogeneous and homogeneous grouping at higher levels. Conant's educational Calvinism leads him to sacrifice some of his concerns for equality of opportunity in favor of a system (somewhat like the British) which he believes will produce the more highly educated leadership needed by our complex society.

Another misconception of Conant that emerged during the heated reactions to *The Education* was that he was derogatorily an "academician," by which it was implied that he was an intellectual snob, unaware of the real problems of living and of public schools, a one-sided bookworm rather than a well-rounded person. (These connotations serve as a counter-stereotype for the "educationist" label which when used with opprobrium implies an anti-intellectual.) Conant's life refutes these views. At Roxbury, he edited the school paper and also played scrub football and served as captain of the second crew. He liked charades and played the female lead in the all-male senior play. His leadership abilities were also exerted as class treasurer and as head of arrangements for the senior class dinner. Golf and mountain-climbing have been among his adult hobbies.

Conant began his studies at Harvard with a $300 scholarship. By proficiency examinations in mathematics and science, he was able to complete his baccalaureate in three years. He studied philosophy with George Santayana, became an honorary John Harvard scholar, and was elected to Phi Beta Kappa and to the *Crimson's* board of editors. But, as the most complete picture currently available of Conant details:

The strenuous demands of the chemistry laboratory, it should be noted in passing, did not smother Conant's enjoyment of college life. With John P. Marquand he developed what was known as the "two-beer dash," a sprint from Miss Mooney's Pleasure Palace [a nickname for the private dormitory where he roomed] via subway, from Harvard Square to Boston and back, drinking the grog in the quickest possible time in the Hub city. He was a fairly regular patron of the stated-Friday-evening parties at Brattle Hall, where subdebs came to dance with documented freshmen. When he moved up to become an upperclassman, he graduated from that group, referred to as "Baby Brats," and pursued the company of the debutantes proper at the regular "Brattle Halls." On occasion, he demonstrated practical skill in handling chemical equipment by such stunts as running a rubber tube from a punch bowl on the table to the mouth of his sleeping roommate Crombie. (At dawn, he remembers, the bowl was empty!) He practiced catching a baseball while standing on a beer barrel, once set up a knight in armor on the third-floor landing of the Pleasure Palace to greet late-returning residents, and on a Christmas holiday traveled with Crombie by coal barge from Providence to Newport News. When the time came, he joined the literary-minded dining club known as the "Signet" where a man was supposed to sit at the table next to "somebody of intelligence." [47]

After his 1913 graduation, Conant went to work for the Midvale Steel Company in Pennsylvania where he learned the electrochemical methods used in steel research. That interest became the basis for his doctoral dissertation, which he completed in 1916 without stopping for a Master's degree. During these studies he also taught chemistry at Harvard. Even before he became Harvard's president, Conant had championed the value of university cooperation with industry and government. Although in *The Citadel of Learning* (1956), he recognized that limits need to be set so that long-range research interests do not suffer from competition with immediately-rewarded ones, he thought both university and society gained from such interaction, regardless of the absences from campus involved in such endeavors. He was not an ivory-tower president; the Harvard faculty's active participation in national affairs has been influenced by Conant's policies.

Conant advocates the clinical professor in education. This is an educator who works part time teaching in the schools and the remaining time supervising interne teachers for the university in the grades and subjects that he teaches. This is entirely consistent with Conant's earlier realist views on the cooperation of higher education with other societal agencies. His analogy to the medical clinical professor and his realization that such a person could not at the same time also be a producer of research (though hopefully would keep abreast of it), shows some flexibility in respect to his ideal of combining research and teaching. Also aware that the present "publish or perish" approach of many universities does not give adequate status or support to such clinical persons, he has stated in respect to that: "I humbly suggest this tradition is completely wrong." [48]

When Conant has been depicted as an aristocrat, his Puritan ancestry has sometimes been cited. Merle Borrowman did not so portray Conant but he did suggest in a short sketch of "Conant, the Man" that some future scholar might place him "as a representative of New England Puritanism in modern dress" in relationship to John Cotton, John Dewey, Charles W. Eliot, and Horace Mann, many of whom also had Unitarian sympathies. [49] In 1943, Conant wrote: "One brand of native American radicalism stems from the barren rocks of the chilly country of the Pilgrim fathers. It might be called individual contrariness." [50] He can trace his ancestry back nine generations on his father's side to Roger Conant, founder of Salem. His mother, Jennette Orr Bryant, was an active Quaker pacifist who traced her lineage back to John Alden of the Mayflower and to William Bradford, Plymouth Colony's second governor. But the Conants were not part of the Cabot, Eliot, and Lowell Boston aristocracy; Conant's immediate family was more middle class. It was not until two years after James Bryant Conant became Harvard's president that he was listed in the *Boston Social Register*. In accord with his philosophy, Conant prides himself on his deeds rather than his lineage. His stress on both achievement and social mobility is consistent with his own upper-middle class background. He values the social elite only to the extent that it has been a responsible and contributing learned aristocracy.

Conant's qualifications to do the study became another issue in the controversy. Some critics of his proposals portrayed him as an outsider to professional education because he lacked any training or degree in professional education. In turn, his supporters pointed out that his accomplishments in the field have so far surpassed many who do have these prerequisites, that he had to be considered an insider by virtue of productivity and length of service. Even Conant's age, seventy at the time of *The Education*'s release, was interpreted as either an asset or a liability; the reprints in this volume illustrate this point. Chapter 3 has some of the positive appellations, and Chapter 5 includes one negative one. In *Saturday Review* (September 19, 1964), Lloyd Pulliam, former chairman of the education department at Knox College, refers to Conant's philosophy as one of "obsolescence" rather than "statesmanship." [51] "Antique," "fossil," "relic" and "senile" have been applied to Conant by persons who differ with his point of view. The nature and level of reaction did not aid in the presentation of alternate positions. As noted in the preface of this book, these kinds of responses also led one educator to write an article expressing his doubts about the possibility of rational debate.

As the discussion turned to more direct concern

with the proposals, the debate over Conant's personal and professional qualifications subsided. But these questions were never squarely faced: Did Conant's experience adequately prepare him to do the teacher education study? What gaps were there in his background? Conant was aware that he had limitations. He used consultants in elementary education, history of education, political science, and teacher education, but those individuals may have been selected in some cases as much for their strong personal and professional characteristics as for their special fields of competency. The final work remained solely Conant's responsibility. Among his strengths were his commitment to a free society, his years of university administrative experience, his long-standing interest and involvement in higher and secondary education, and his personal and professional integrity. He seems to have tried to be impartial and scientifically objective. While *The Education* was being discussed, Conant was serving as a Ford Foundation sponsored advisor to the education officials of West Berlin. He was especially involved in the development of a new European pedagogical center located in West Berlin. He has also served as vice-chairman of the President's Commission on Youth Employment.[52]

Conant's background seems weakest in the lack of direct teaching and other experiences at the elementary and secondary school levels. He has been least concerned with elementary education and appears not to consider school policies in relation to child growth and human development (except for ability), as much as in relationship to societal consequences and administrative arrangements. He views the earlier stages of schooling as they relate to the later ones and to higher education. Conant very seldom, if ever, discusses children in his writing. He did recommend that all teachers have an elementary course in psychology and has also suggested that a course in educational psychology, including child psychology, would be a desirable university requirement for elementary teachers. In the late thirties, he mentioned (without being more specific) advances in child growth and development along with those in the study of administrative problems and in ability testing as examples of major progress in professional education.

An intermediary professor is one who works in an academic subject, field, or area as applied to professional education. Although Conant recommends that intermediary professors be trained in one of the more applicable academic disciplines (for him, history, philosophy, political science, psychology, and sociology), he does not have this training. He has neither had nor does he recommend any training in professional education for intermediary professors. Yet, because of his numerous educational activities, Conant is definitely less of a layman in professional education than Abraham Flexner was in medicine when he undertook his Carnegie-sponsored study of medical education published in 1910. Several reviews compared their reports, but Flexner was selected because he was a medical layman. According to John S. Hollister, Conant's project administrator at Educational Testing Service, "Mr. Education" was not selected as a layman and did not consciously pattern his study after Flexner's.[53]

Another major issue was whether Conant's study was strictly empirical and scientific, or whether he used his data to build a case (having seen and discovered what he expected) to confirm his prior opinions. Conant made both firm recommendations and personal suggestions. The work has a normative as well as a descriptive aspect. Unlike John Dewey, Conant does not integrate the theoretical-deductive and empirical-inductive approaches to form one all-embracing scientific method. Conant conceives of science as involving both distinctive modes of thought, each having its advantages and disadvantages. Both Dewey and Conant share a commitment to science, although each defines it and its scope somewhat differently. Scientist Conant is more skeptical (an attitude he identifies with science) about the application of scientific methods to nonempirical value areas than was philosopher Dewey, but again, their conceptions of science are different. Healthy, not cynical, skepticism and tolerance for diverse views are traits both Dewey and Conant have frequently endorsed. Both believe it is possible to obtain predictive generalizations in the social sciences, but much more difficult than in the natural or physical sciences. Yet, Conant avoided exposing the deductive aspects of his recommendations and suggestions in *The Education*.

For Conant, the test of truth is not merely general and pragmatic—operational consequences and success—but is also, more specifically, the production of further theory and scientific inquiry: "Science is a dynamic undertaking directed to lowering the degree of empiricism involved in solving problems; or if you prefer, science is a process of fabricating a web of interconnected concepts and conceptual schemes arising from experiments and observations and fruitful of further experiments and observations." [54] While sharing Dewey's stress on consequences, Conant defines them more concretely. Conant also opposes utility as the chief reason for seeking truth, having quoted Michael Faraday's response to a woman who asked why he was conducting certain experiments: "Madam, what is the use of a baby?" [55] Like Dewey, Conant does not consider science to be merely sensory empiricism: "Science is a speculative enterprise" and "The history of science demonstrates beyond a doubt that the really revolutionary and significant advances come not from empiricism but from new theories." [56]

In education, realist Conant has stressed few theories, and one of these has been "practice before theory." While Conant favors and uses both deductive rationalism and inductive empiricism, he wrote in 1959: "Over the years I have wrestled with definitions and struggled with chains of logical reasoning; I have been guilty of my share of educational banalities. As a consequence, I must confess to an increasing distrust of the use of the deductive method of thinking about questions confronting teachers." [57] Scientist Conant has generally spoken for demonstration methods of proof over merely verbal ones, and examples and illustrations to clarify definitions. He suspects that words are too frequently mistaken for reality. In one of his early speeches to Harvard freshmen, he warned them to be wary of such easy labeling as "Bourbon" or "Communist" and of "words used in a perfectly meaningless manner" such as "psychology, integration, relativity, complexes, vitamins, service." [58]

Conant states that any single world philosophy or theology is reductive. He claims no single orientation himself, and tends to dislike and even deny labels attached to his outlook, except perhaps the empirical or Jeffersonian ones. In 1964, he wrote:

I doubt if anyone will challenge the statement that the influence of the German philosophic tradition which starts with Kant is less than it was two or three generations ago.

Indeed, in the United States it is hard to find today admirers of the writings of Hegel, and most people have forgotten if they ever knew, that John Dewey started as an Hegelian. The retreat of systematic philosophy has paralleled the advance of the natural sciences.[59]

Conant favors analytical rather than systematic philosophy and holds that education approached on the basis of a single cosmology or metaphysics, be it Marxism, Thomism, pragmatism, existentialism or any other "ism," leads to indoctrination. Yet, his own realist "nonmetaphysical" temperament challenges both the philosophies of pure idealism and of pragmatism of American educators. He has sought to foster full academic freedom at Harvard and elsewhere so that conflicting positions may freely compete. He believes these are the basic requisites of both science and education in an open society, but in education he seldom focuses directly on alternate positions. His political effectiveness in the education arena seems enhanced by that strategy and tactic, while his intellectual contribution is diminished. Only his *Two Modes of Thought* (1964) dealt directly with his underlying philosophy of education. While this may be his most significant and lasting treatise on education, it has generally failed to win notice from the American public and educators who have been so aroused by the currency, concreteness, and immediacy of Conant's more practically-focused education volumes.

James Van Patten's "A Search for Substance in Conant's Educational Writings" (*The Journal of Teacher Education*, June 1965) failed to connect Conant's educational views with his scientific and social philosophy and therefore discovered little. This was partly due to

Van Patten's limiting himself to Conant's writings on education. While Conant grants the relationship between one's social philosophy and one's educational positions, he has seldom made explicit connections in his own stands. In most of his education works, they remain implicit. He focuses attention instead on specific proposals that appear to be developed inductively rather than derived even partially from his assumed social ideology. He avoids debating his social ideology probably because he considers it to be more an assertion of personal opinions and values than a judgment of facts. As a realist, he tries to separate facts and values, but then he presents his recommendations as though they were simply the results of facts. Pragmatists are divided on the connection between facts and values. Dewey was not entirely clear on this either. John L. Childs has stressed their relationship, while Bruce R. Raup and others have emphasized their distinctiveness.[60]

Both Conant and Dewey have favored learning from experience, with a connection between the direct and cognitive aspects. Dewey stressed their integral links more than Conant whose emphasis is that direct experience and practice should be prior to theory. For opposing a state's requiring education-theory courses before teaching, Conant was accused of being against theory, as he had previously been attacked as being nonmetaphysical. He has suggested that German education suffers from an overemphasis on theory, and has championed the case-method approach of training lawyers and businessmen as well as teachers of history, especially history of the sciences. His stress on practical experience accompanies his expressed predilection for induction and the case-method of teaching. By that means, a specific event, such as the depression or a war, or a discovery, such as Boyle's laws of gas pressures or Alexander Graham Bell's invention of the telephone, is studied. In the case of events, an effort is made to determine causation, and with discoveries and inventions, to examine the particular derivation of a scientific method, fact, theory, or technological contribution. From these specific cases, generalizations are supposed to be inductively derived.

In line with his philosophy of science, Conant employs both the deductive and inductive modes in his teacher-education study. While appearing more inductive and more cautiously limited in its application than the Deweyan view of science, Conant's conception is as broad:

If the preceding analysis of history be correct, Petrarch, Boccaccio, Machiavelli, and Erasmus, far more than the alchemists, must be considered the spiritual precursors of the modern scientific investigator. Likewise, Rabelais and Montaigne who carried forward the critical philosophic spirit must be counted among the forerunners of the modern scientists. Not only the Renaissance antiquarians, and a few hardy sceptics, but also honest explorers and hard-headed statesmen were the ancestors of all who have since endeavored to find new answers to old questions, who desire to minimize prejudice and examine facts impartially. As I see it, scientists today represent the progeny of one line of descent who migrated, so to speak, some centuries ago into certain fields which were ripe for cultivation.[61]

The Education was in accord with both this spirit and Conant's earlier predispositions, which he did not seem to find empirically contradicted by his supposed sense-realist concern with data.

Whether scientific method consists of the two separate modes of theoretical deductive rationalism and inductive empiricism, or whether it is a combination of these modes, is not simply an academic matter. The structure and organization of the educators of teachers is involved. There is presently a division in the field of education between intermediary professors who see their role as bringing to the field of education the contributions of their particular academic disciplines and those who see themselves as educational researchers in their own right. The former tend to rely too heavily on the deductive mode, and the latter overly stress empiricism. There are even two competing professional organizations, the older (1906) National Society of College Teachers of Education (NSCTE), whose members tend to stress generalist, theoretical, societal, and intermediary concerns, and the newer (1915) American Educational Research Association (AERA), whose members stress specific empirical studies. One impact of science on education can be seen in the phenomenal growth of AERA, while NSCTE has wrestled in recent years with maintaining itself and redefining its national role. A new organization loosely affiliated with NSCTE, the American Educational Studies Association (AESA), is more rationally and societally oriented than the more technologically directed AERA.

So far, only a few outstanding educators have bridged the gap between AERA and NSCTE (which now includes AESA), but there has been some discussion of at least one combined session at each of their now annual meetings, which since 1966 have not been held concurrently. As AERA broadens to include more of the theoretical, historical, philosophical, societal, and international aspects of education, it is possible that the two modes might become combined in a truly "research" organization. AERA might also become the American Educationist Association for those educationists who seek a professional society like the American Psychological Association. As NSCTE redefines its role to focus specifically on teacher education rather than on being an umbrella group for the different intermediary professors, the character of its membership should change to include more empiricists as well as rationalists. Then, both organizations could have greater communication between those holding to the "two modes," and there could be more explorations of the possible interrelationships and complementary aspects of these modes by those who currently hold unilaterally to only one or the other of these approaches to knowledge, and who, like Conant, conceive of these modes as entirely separate. If NSCTE can successfully bring together the resources of AERA and AESA, the split between the technologically- and societally-oriented educators (predicted for the year 2,000 by William Van Til, Coffman Distinguished Professor in Education at Indiana State University), might be avoided.[62]

It seems odd, however, that Conant does not require clinical experience of intermediary professors although he does require it of their students. Such professors, then, may have the purist research advantage of constructing theories and studies without concern for relevancy or use. It seems, however, that they would be at a disadvantage in demonstrating to their students the relevancy of their disciplines to the practicalities of the students' actual teaching situations. Conant's proposals of heavily clinically experienced professors and academically-trained theoretical intermediary professors appear to follow from his bifurcation of scientific method into the two separate modes of inductive empiricism and deductive rationalism. From this writer's perspective, this merely continues the present divorce between practitioners who know too little research and theory, and academic educationalists who know too little of the clinical and practical. Whether the modes are seen as separate or as related, both the clinician and academician in education need the "two modes of thought." More appreciation, communication, and cooperation among academicians and clinicians is necessary in education, as in other fields.

One criticism of *The Education* was that many of Conant's ideas were not new to him, thus indicating that he had used the deductive mode more than the inductive. One critical *non sequitur* was that merely because his views were old, they were not relevant. Within three years after assuming Harvard's presidency, Conant pioneered an interdisciplinary Master of Arts in teaching degree for those who wanted to do graduate work related to secondary school teaching. As early as his 1937–1938 report to the Board of Overseers, Conant had written:

It is, perhaps, not an overstatement to say that, by and large, American universities have avoided a wholehearted systematic attention to public education at the school level. Certainly there has rarely been, in any institution, a concerted attack by the faculties of arts and sciences and of education on the problems presented by the new conditions [the expansion of secondary schools into mass rather than selective institutions]. Yet such an effort is imperatively needed. There is no question today that the study of education as a social process—quite apart from the training of teachers—is as important as the study of law or of business administration. Any university which wishes to do its share for the public welfare must have a strong faculty of education with the same degree of professional feelings as exists in other professional faculties.[63]

Those who were concerned about his elimination of state-required education theory courses in the preparation of teachers too readily assumed that he did not value such courses at all. While he questions their inclusion as prerequisites to the field, Conant says they are desirable as university research areas and graduate electives for students who have had prior teaching experience. This seems to result directly from his view that practice should precede theory rather than the reverse German pattern. In other words, it is his belief that certain theoretical learning occurs best when preceded by primary experiences to which it can be related.

One real advantage of teaching experience before studying intermediary theory and research is that prior to successful teaching, students often have so many fears about such specific teaching tasks as classroom discipline that to involve them in the broader liberal, social, and psychological aspects before they have some classroom security is to waste learning time. Their main concerns and interests must first be met. It is not sufficient to merely have prior teaching experience; the experience must be of the kind that will build confidence and lead the student to want to explore some of the less immediate and more abstract intricacies of his chosen field. With some modifications and some quality stipulations, Conant's plan in this regard could enhance the maturity of the learner and increase the effectiveness of teacher education. But experience, *per se*, no more guarantees increased maturity and the ability to cope with large questions than does the aging process. In this writer's experience as a teacher, the personality of the student, especially in respect to emotional and intellectual security, open versus closed mindedness, and flexibility versus rigidity, is as crucial to their readiness to explore the societal and theoretical aspects of education as is their age or amount of teaching experience. Testing this point recently in a foundations class I was teaching, I found no difference between perception of the relevancy of foundations material on an area such as social-class factors by those who had previously student-taught and those who had not. In fact, in that class those who had student teaching were more closed in their perceptions of what teaching is all about.

While some educators and psychologists have asserted that bright high school youth can work with abstract ideas, Conant maintains that theoretical education courses require the greater maturity of an older, more experienced student. Conant's view on these courses suggests they be studied on a purely voluntary basis. As previously explained, from this writer's perspective, theoretical studies might follow practice, but if they are significant areas of study they should be required by institutions (if not by the state). There could still be a choice among courses from the several different intermediary humanities and social sciences as they are applied to the study of education, and thus, also among different teachers and disciplines. In some places, an eclectic "foundations" course serves this function for all students. But if prospective or practicing teachers are to become professional to the extent of understanding education in its widest social sense, as Conant has himself acknowledged and as Lawrence A. Cremin proposed in his *The Wonderful World of Ellwood Patterson Culberley* (1965), it seems that more than just the study of only one of the following will be necessary: anthropology of education, comparative education, economics of education, history of education, philosophy of education, politics of education, and sociology of education. Would it be too much to require prospective teachers to study at least two of the above subjects and all college students to study one?

Conant's desire that both liberal arts and education professors cooperate in the education of teachers goes back at least to his instituting the M.A.T. as a "joint enterprise." He hints in that 1937–1938 report of the need for what has since been termed the "all-university" commitment:

For both the training of teachers and the study of educational problems at the school level have become too much divorced from the university atmosphere in almost all parts of the country. The university schools of education have been too concerned with quantity production, too anxious to further their own disciplines by legislative enactments requiring of all teachers courses in education. They have been for the most part teachers' colleges—vocational institutions—with only a formal allegiance (if any) to the community of scholars which constitute a university.[64]

At the same time, Conant pointed out that the new program was designed to be a more difficult one than the older ones and thus could not be expected to bring the increase of enrollments or income that would provide for the expansion of education faculty and research: "This degree, since it requires the certification by one faculty of accomplishment in the subject which is later to be taught and a certificate by another faculty of fitness for teaching (determined by apprenticeship and examinations on educational problems) is rarely attained in one year. It is intentionally a degree with high standards." [65] One of the basic problems in teacher education has been the loss of enrollment in high-level institutions that attempt to raise standards by developing more difficult programs; many students gravitate to institutions having curricula that are easier to complete. But, as Paul Woodring outlined in *New Directions in Teacher Education* (1957), the "newer" patterns that appear to be effective, such as the Master of Arts in Teaching (M.A.T.), one-year programs that combine liberal and professional study after a four-year liberal arts undergraduate program, eventually become models for other colleges and universities. The elevating of standards in one institution may help to raise them in others if what seems to succeed in a high-standard institution can work in an average or low-standard one. Consciously or not, many state colleges are currently testing this theory in their recent upgrading attempts, but one problem with the M.A.T. programs is that they are being used to strengthen the enrollment in academic courses on the untested premise that by such means teacher effectiveness will be improved. Often, their real purpose is to aid in the transforming of state colleges with high teacher education enrollments into liberal arts institutions.

Conant has long condemned the academic man for not being more concerned with the training of teachers and the study of education in its widest social-process meaning, not merely in its school sense. The fact that academic men merely complained about what they did not like in terms of mass mediocre education led Conant to write in his first book on education in 1948:

Historically the liberal arts colleges abdicated, and teachers colleges and schools of education took over the job. They

were the inheritors of the separatist tradition of the earlier
normal schools. When university professors blame the
schools of education for the shortcomings of our public
schools, the reply from the professors of education in historical terms is all too evident. But while the origin of the
quarrel is of significance, the important matter is not to
assess blame but to work for close cooperation in the
future.[66]

It would follow then for Conant, that the intermediary professor should first of all be schooled in his academic discipline and then primarily interested, though
not necessarily trained, in the study of education. His
reluctance to affirm education directly as a science
seems to relate to his belief that as an applied field, like
engineering or medicine, it must rely on other sciences.
He seems to have changed to this position from his earlier view of education as a social science. However, this
may only appear a shift because his later focus was on
teacher education rather than on the study of education
as a social process. He does not see a necessary (as contrasted with a desirable) connection between teacher
preparation and the study of education. This may relate
to his assumption that the prime role of the teacher is
to be the developer of competency and depth in a subject field. He recommended subject majors for teachers
of grades four and up.

The Education was not strictly an empirical study
or merely a deductive polemic. Conant's conclusions
came in the form of prescriptive statements rather than
descriptive or predictive generalizations. They could not
be proved or disproved by the study alone. Hence, both
disputes and further investigations have ensued. Conant's recommendations and suggestions are generally
consistent with his socioeducational philosophy and in

many cases are not newly formulated by him. Historical precedents can be found for many of his ideas such as institutional recommendation of teachers. This might be traced to Johann Bernard Basedow who founded a German teacher education seminary along Rousseauian principles in the late eighteenth century. Basedow declared:

An examination helps to find good teachers only if they are there, but it does not educate a number of them. For this purpose seminaries are necessary. There must therefore be in each country a teacher training school in which are pupils with whom to work and in which young men who desire to enter schoolteaching are under the supervision of experienced professors of education and complete their training years. Toward the end of their training the institution can give a testimonial that gives the chooser of the teachers more information than an examination. . . .[67]

Of course Basedow was thinking of smaller institutions than the university complexes of twentieth-century America.

The charges that Conant's ideas are not completely new or totally original or solely the result of empirical studies might be made of such other noted educational leaders as Thomas Jefferson, Horace Mann, or John Dewey. Like Jefferson and Mann, Conant is primarily a political statesman advocating innovations to secure his socioeducational ideals. All three can be viewed as educational pioneers and political planners building on inherited ideas frequently initiated and developed by others. While Dewey also built upon the ideas of others and was concerned with achieving actual changes in practice, he was most actively involved in developing and reevaluating the then new, pragmatic educational theory. Dewey was mainly concerned with practice as a way of testing theory for its operational consequences; he stressed theory for its personal and social usefulness. Conant is an educational theoretician, but as a realist he questions the importance of theory to education. Dewey was a trained philosopher whose pragmatic belief was that the most important and most practical endeavors were theoretical ones. While Conant includes philosophy among the academic subjects to be examined for inclusion in curricula for prospective teachers, he mentions that field last; math and physical sciences are first and second on Conant's list.

Conant's questioning of the value of psychology or philosophy taught at a young age recalls the arguments by the advocates of the old and new math, questioning which can be taught earlier. We need experiments in this area of education, not just pronouncements that *appear* to be the results of scientific investigation. In taking abstract positions in contrast to Conant's concrete ones, Dewey blurred differences so as to encourage and simulate agreement among educators, some of whom were in effect pursuing vastly different courses of action. Dewey later sharply condemned some of these alternatives for which his support was claimed. Dewey sought consensus at the general level, but he is not always perfectly clear. Conant's specificity has been greater than that of John Dewey. Conant thus fosters both more clarity and more disagreement than Dewey.

The teacher education controversy focused on only some of Conant's recommendations: elimination of state certification requirements except practice teaching; the all-university or interdepartmental approach; the clinical professorship; opposition to lengthening the initial preparatory-school period; depth subject matter emphasis (especially for upper-elementary teachers); and criticism of the existing composition and power of the National Council for the Accrediting of Teacher Education (NCATE).

Many of his recommendations were minimally controversial among professional education leadership: the state information services, state-controlled assignment of teachers by local boards, certification reciprocity, state aid for practice teaching, loan policy for future teachers, selection of cooperating teachers, induction proposals for new teachers, salary scale suggestions, state financial aid for summer school and leaves of absence for further study by teachers, in-service education of teachers, and adequate staffing by small colleges.

Other recommendations were questioned but were not central to the controversy: preparing art, music, and physical education teachers for all levels of schooling; a single-field diploma for secondary school teachers; and no credit for courses taken while teaching full time. Criticisms of specific proposals were sometimes countered with the argument that they should be seen in relationship to the others, but any hope that the *total* plan would be acceptable to all or anyone except Conant himself could only be termed utopian. Conant's successful career results partly from his being a political realist. He is concerned with being effective, and attempts only what he deems feasible and possible of fruition. To criticize him simply for that, as some have done, would be to praise failure.

If only on the basis of his immense activity in the field and his enormous audience and impact, Conant, the educator, deserves far more extensive and analytical consideration in the history and philosophy of education than he has received. The need for careful evaluation of Conant's positions becomes even more crucial when one considers that his general approach represents dominant American conceptions in the 1960s. As noted earlier in this chapter, Conant's general orientation seems to be shared by John W. Gardner, among others. Conant's traditional outlook not only received support from the current culture but also aid from government and foundations. It fits our "Great Society" with its immense strengths and its glaring defects. This view may help explain the extremes of the favorable and the unfavorable responses to Conant's work.

As Lawrence A. Cremin pointed out in *The Transformation of the School* (1961), vast social changes will have to await a new era of social reform. Americans have been concerned with maintaining their economic and political superiority as a technologically-advanced power in a world of cold wars and limited-fighting wars. These wars affect not only those directly involved, but also harm many domestic education programs by diverting funds away from such crucial agencies as the Office of Economic Opportunity (OEO), the Department of Health, Education, and Welfare (HEW), and the Department of Labor. The present situation of militarism abroad and militant racism at home has increased the need for critical assessments of our society such as have been made by peace groups, students protesting antiquated college orientations, and those seeking power for the black minority of our nation.

In American culture, with its so-called liberal education, men are very often the opposite of what they appear, or even consider themselves to be. Public relations mask inner truths. A genuinely liberal education should be concerned with more than appearances. Fear of personal exposure and of intimacy threatens our society and the many hidden selves who comprise it. Henry Thoreau stated, "Nothing is so much to be feared as fear." Franklin Delano Roosevelt said, "The only thing we have to fear is fear itself." John F. Kennedy declared, "I think we can do better—we have to do better. . . . I do not accept the view that our high noon is past. Our brightest days can be ahead." When educators (academicians and educationists) once again focus on the basic problems of the individual person in today's world, liberal education will not have to be defended. It will permeate our way of life and thus our schools at all levels. Teacher education will then be the concern of even more Americans who care about youth as individuals and as architects and as inhabitants of a future social system.

We need to face, as Conant does, that this permeation is not a reality at present, and then devise not only practical but also much more stimulating approaches to accelerating change in that direction. To improve the culture is a more encompassing and complex challenge than merely concentrating on teacher education narrowly defined. As Conant has himself indicated in his writings about Germany, improving teacher education or any professional preparation as such not only does not guarantee a free society but may even be a factor in its downfall. This is especially true if one thinks of education too separately from the culture and its values. A better culture will, by virtue of all the experiences it affords, have a better education of teachers. The question of how best to educate teachers is linked to how best to educate the children they will teach and the answer to that lies in some conception of the kind of adults we want them to be. This necessitates a vision of a desirable society.

Conant's recommendations fail to deal with these important and basic matters. He leaves the impression that, for him, American society is generally desirable with a few minor changes needed. If mass media reflect popular American culture, much radical change is urgently needed, even if not demanded by those whose education and culture have taught them to be too satisfied with the superficial but often impoverishing riches and rituals of American life. We need only to think of the problems in our cities or the problem of drugs and mental health to confirm this need for considerable social improvement. Teacher education needs to be assessed in relationship to the challenges to education and to teachers our societal conditions and needs impart, that is, as part of the larger cultural context within which education takes place and is defined and evaluated.

Conant recently raised the question of the relevancy of Jeffersonianism for contemporary American society and education. We may ask, what is the significance today of Conant's approach? To wrestle with the issues posed by the Conant controversy in teacher education is to face the complexities involved in the basic underlying questions of American socioeducational policy. Despite the Conant study, we still do not know the best way to educate teachers. "Best" must be defined in terms of social and philosophical conceptions of the goals of life and of education. Our society emphasizes means and "how" rather than aims, ends, and "why." Americans generally have separate rather than integrated idealist and materialist conceptions; we debate implementation. Our scientific, technological culture and Conant's realism accept this. That is why our society values practical, technique-minded, empirically-oriented researchers in organizations, including schools. That is also why many intellectuals in the field of education are looked down upon by both practitioners and academicians. There is anti-intellectualism in American education practiced by both those unconcerned with the application of knowledge and those concerned only with that which is useful. Conant's separatist and hierarchical position on pure and applied knowledge and his overly cautious approaches to the education field partially mirror and sustain this anti-intellectual attitude which frequently masquerades as intellectualism.

The need today is not just for both the deductive and inductive modes (theory and empiricism), but also for critical and scholarly evaluations of both in relation to the present social matrix. The hope, as always, lies with youth. They will not necessarily be able to change the total culture but they can at least be educated to understand it and to refuse to accept all aspects of it as deserving of continuance merely because these aspects exist. The ideal of improving our culture will help it to flourish, not merely survive. By seeking very temperate gradual changes, realist Conant discreetly contributes to social improvement, but his wariness may be serving to delay even those social changes which he deems necessary.

Notes

1. Merle Borrowman, "Conant, the Man," *Saturday Review*, September 21, 1963, p. 58.
2. Quoted by Roy A. Edelfelt in his "Foreword" to "A

Symposium on James Bryant Conant's *The Education of American Teachers.*" *The Journal of Teacher Education* (March 1964), 5. The quote is also reprinted in *Saturday Review*, September 19, 1964, p. 62.

3. James B. Conant, "Who Should Go to College?" *Ladies' Home Journal*, June 1948, p. 106.

4. James E. McClellan, "James Bryant Conant: A Man-Made System and Vice-Versa," in *Toward an Effective Critique of American Education* (Philadelphia: Lippincott, 1968), pp. 59–127. McClellan concludes, "I have given reasons for holding that, in relation to this vision of things, Conant has not provided and could not provide rationally compelling arguments for educational policy," p. 118.

5. Quoted in Luella Cole, *A History of Education: Socrates to Montessori* (New York: Rinehart, 1950), p. 274.

6. Quoted in Newton Edwards and Herman G. Richey, *The School in the American Social Order*, 2nd ed. (Boston: Houghton Mifflin, 1963), p. 371.

7. Merle Borrowman, "Liberal Education and the Professional Preparation of Teachers," in Merle Borrowman, ed., *Teacher Education in America: A Documentary History* (New York: Teachers College Press, 1965), pp. 38–39, 51 ff.

8. James B. Conant, *Education in a Divided World: The Function of the Public Schools in Our Unique Society* (Cambridge, Mass.: Harvard University Press, 1948), p. 159. For Hutchins' views, see *The Conflict in Education* (New York: Harper & Row, 1953); *Education for Freedom* (Baton Rouge: Louisiana State University Press, 1943); *The Higher Learning in America* (New Haven: Yale University Press, 1936); and *The University of Utopia* (Chicago: University of Chicago Press, 1933). Bestor's philosophy appears in *Educational Wastelands* (Urbana: University of Illinois Press, 1953); and *The Restoration of Learning: A*

Program for Redeeming the Unfulfilled Promise of American Education (New York: Knopf, 1955). Koerner's views are found in *The Case for Basic Education: A Program of Aims for Public Schools* (Boston: Little, Brown, 1959); and *The Miseducation of American Teachers* (Boston: Houghton Mifflin, 1963). Kerr's ideas are stated in *The Uses of the University* (Cambridge, Mass.: Harvard University Press, 1964).

9. James B. Conant, untitled address delivered January 27, 1950, at the symposium "Functions of a Modern University," *Proceedings of the First Symposium Sponsored by State University of New York* (Albany: State University of New York, 1950), p. 13.

10. James B. Conant, unpublished, untitled speech delivered November 1, 1939 to the University of Missouri Convocation, Conant Papers, Harvard University Archives, HUH 298, Box two, p. 8.

11. James B. Conant, "The Future of our Higher Education," *Harpers Magazine*, May 1938, p. 570.

12. From the annual report of James B. Conant, President of Harvard University to the Board of Overseers as reprinted in "Reports: The Aim of Harvard University," *School and Society*, XXXII (February 3, 1934), 147.

13. Paul F. Douglass, *Six Upon the World: Toward an American Culture for an Industrial Age* (Boston: Little, Brown, 1954), p. 418. In Douglass, see also, Chap. VI, "James B. Conant: Emergence of a Coherent and Unified Culture for Free Men," pp. 326–409, the Introduction, and the concluding chapter.

14. Conant, "Who Should Go to College?" *op cit.*, p. 111.

15. James B. Conant, "Harvard, Present and Future," *School and Society*, XLIII (April 4, 1936), 451–452.

16. James B. Conant, *Germany and Freedom* (Cambridge, Mass.: Harvard University Press, 1958), p. 3.

17. James B. Conant, *Two Modes of Thought: My Encounters with Science and Education* (New York: Trident Press, 1964), p. xxvii.

18. Conant, *Proceedings of the First Symposium Sponsored by State University of New York, op. cit.*, pp. 15–16.

19. Conant, *Germany and Freedom, op. cit.*, pp. 4–5.

20. *Ibid.*, p. 30.

21. James B. Conant, "President's Report 1936–37," January 10, 1938, *Official Register of Harvard University*, XXV (February 19, 1938), 6. See also, *A Statement by the Cambridge Union of University Teachers Concerning President Conant's Annual Report*, February 14, 1938, in Harvard University, Widener Library.

22. Conant, "The Future of Our Higher Education," *op. cit.*, p. 565.

23. Conant, "Who Should Go to College," *op. cit.*, p. 113; James B. Conant, *The Citadel of Learning* (New Haven: Yale University Press, 1956), p. 70; Conant, *Education in a Divided World, op. cit.*, pp. 156–157, 202; and "Dr. James B. Conant Answers Questions You Ask About the Schools," *Changing Times*, XX (January 1966), 29.

24. James B. Conant, *Thomas Jefferson and the Development of American Public Education* (Berkeley: University of California Press, 1963), p. 56.

25. James B. Conant, "Teacher Certification: The Restricted State Approved Program Approach," in *The Education of American Teachers*, paperback edition, (New York: McGraw-Hill, 1964), p. 244.

26. Borrowman, *Teacher Education in the United States, op. cit.*, p. 219.

27. Robert H. Beck in "A Symposium on James Bryant Conant's *The Education of American Teachers*," *op. cit.*, p. 44. See also Albert Jay Nock, *The Theory of Education in the United States* (New York: Harcourt Brace & World, 1932).

28. James B. Conant, "Wanted: American Radicals," *Atlantic Monthly*, May 1943, p. 43.

29. Alexander Lincoln, *Where Does Harvard Now Stand? Some Critical Thoughts* (Boston: Privately printed for the author, 1944). This is to be found in Harvard University's Widener Library.

30. M. Whitcomb Hess, "Conant's Big-Business Fascism," *Catholic World*, April 1953, p. 26.

31. Oliver Martin, *Two Educators: Hutchins and Conant* (Hinsdale, Ill.: Regnery, 1948), p. 4. See also "The Human Affairs Pamphlets," Pamphlet #29, pp. 19–25, available at Harvard University, Widener Library.

32. Conant, "Wanted: American Radicals," *op. cit.*, p. 43.

33. John H. Chafee, Jr., and editorial "Conant Plan Haste," *Boston Sunday Herald*, August 22, 1965, Section 4, p. 6; "Conant's Plan Draws Fire," *Boston Sunday Herald*, August 22, 1965, Section 6, p. 1; for the full compact, see Herman I. Orentlicher, "The Compact for Education: A Proposal for Shaping Nationwide Educational Policy," *AAUP Bulletin*, CI (December 1965), 437–446.

34. Richard Wynn, "An Inept Lesson in Educational Policy Making," *Phi Delta Kappan*, XLVI (February 1965), 251–256; and Paul Nash, "Conant's Shaping Educational Policy," *Graduate Journal*, XV (1966–67), 36.

35. Franklin Parker, "The Interstate Compact," *Changing Education*, I (Spring 1966), 33.

36. James B. Conant, "Liberal Education: The Selective Principle in American Colleges," *Vital Speeches of the Day* (February 1, 1937), pp. 254, 256.

37. Van Cleve Morris, *Philosophy and the American School* (Boston: Houghton Mifflin, 1961), p. 381.

38. Conant, *Education in a Divided World*, *op. cit.*, p. 145.

39. James B. Conant, "Education for a Classless Society: The Jeffersonian Tradition," *Atlantic Monthly*, May 1940, p. 600.

40. Fred M. Hechinger, "Conant Reports School Financing in 'Chaotic State,'" *The New York Times*, February 26, 1967, p. 60.
41. James B. Conant, "The Function of the Secondary School and College in Educating for Social and Cultural Leadership," School and Society, XLI (January 5, 1935), 1.
42. Quoted in Douglass, *op. cit.*, p. 332.
43. Willis Rudy, *Schools in an Age of Mass Culture: An Exploration of Selected Themes in the History of Twentieth-Century American Education* (Englewood Cliffs, N. J.: Prentice-Hall, 1965), p. 235.
44. Conant, *Education in a Divided World, op. cit.*, p. 235.
45. Conant, "Liberal Education: The Selective Principle in American Colleges," *op. cit.*, p. 255.
46. Morris, *op. cit.*, pp. 214, 340.
47. Douglass, *op. cit.*, pp. 334–335.
48. Conant, "Teacher Certification: The Restricted State Approved Program Approach," *op. cit.*, pp. 234–235.
49. Borrowman, "Conant, the Man," *loc. cit.*
50. Conant, "Wanted: American Radicals," *op. cit.*, p. 44.
51. Lloyd Pulliam, "Statesmanship and Obsolescence," *Saturday Review*, September 19, 1964, pp. 54–55, and 72–74.
52. James B. Altbach, "James B. Conant, Educator," *Phi Delta Kappan*, XLV (October 1963), 12.
53. See, among others, Donald W. Robinson's "Education's Flexner Report," *Phi Delta Kappan*, XLV (June 1964), pp. 426–432. For information about Flexner, see his *Do Americans Really Value Education?* (Cambridge, Mass.: Harvard University Press, 1927); and *Abraham Flexner: An Autobiography* (N. Y.: Simon and Schuster, 1960). The information about Conant's not being selected as a layman was on p. 2 of a letter dated May 6, 1965 to this writer from John S. Hollister, identified in the preface to this book.

54. James B. Conant, *Modern Science and Modern Man* (Garden City, N. Y.: Doubleday Anchor Books, 1953), pp. 106–107.

55. James B. Conant, "Friends and Enemies of Learning," *The Yale Review*, XXV (March 1936), 475.

56. James B. Conant, *Science and Common Sense* (New Haven: Yale University Press, 1951), p. 25; and Conant, *Modern Science and Modern Man, op. cit.*, p. 53.

57. James B. Conant, *The Child, the Parent, and the State* (Cambridge, Mass.: Harvard University Press, 1960), p. 1.

58. James B. Conant, "The College Years," *School and Society* (September 29, 1934), p. 429.

59. Conant, *Two Modes of Thought, op. cit.*, pp. 82–83.

60. See John L. Childs, Education and Morals (New York: Appleton Century-Crofts, 1950); and Bruce L. Raup *et al., The Improvement of Practical Intelligence: The Central Task of Education* (New York: Harper & Row, 1950).

61. James B. Conant, *On Understanding Science: A Historical Approach* (New Haven: Yale University Press, 1947), p. 9.

62. William Van Til, "The Year 2000: Teacher Education" (Terre Haute: Indiana State University, 1968), pp. 33–35. Monograph.

63. From the annual report of James B. Conant, President of Harvard University to the Board of Overseers, as reprinted in "The University and the High School," *School and Society*, XLIX (February 11, 1939), 164.

64. *Ibid.*, p. 165.

65. *Ibid.*, p. 166.

66. Conant, *Education in a Divided World, op. cit.*, p. 147.

67. Quoted in Cole, *op. cit.*, p. 417.

2

The Famous
Twenty-Seven

James B. Conant

For KAPPAN readers who have not read the latest Conant report, here are the twenty-seven recommendations which are usually regarded as the heart of *The Education of American Teachers*. In a recent letter to KAPPAN editors, Mr. Conant said that he would like Recommendations 11, 24, 25, and 26 to receive more emphasis than they have been accorded in the more than 2,000 reviews that have appeared in this country to date.

GROUP A RECOMMENDATIONS REQUIRING ACTION EITHER BY A CHIEF STATE SCHOOL OFFICER, A STATE BOARD OF EDUCATION, OR A LEGISLATURE

1. *Certification requirements.* For certification purposes the state should require only (a) that a candi-

date hold a baccalaureate degree from a legitimate college or university, (b) that he submit evidence of having successfully performed as a student teacher under the direction of college and public school personnel in whom the state department has confidence, and in a practice-teaching situation of which the state department approves, and (c) that he hold a specially endorsed teaching certificate from a college or university which, in issuing the official document, attests that the institution as a whole considers the person adequately prepared to teach in a designated field and grade level.

5. *Programs of practice teaching.* The state should approve programs of practice teaching. It should, working cooperatively with the college and public school authorities, regulate the conditions under which practice teaching is done and the nature of the methods instruction that accompanies it. The state should require that the colleges and public school systems involved submit evidence concerning the competence of those appointed as cooperating teachers and clinical professors.

6. *State information service.* State departments of education should develop and make available to local school boards and colleges and universities data relevant to the preparation and employment of teachers. Such data may include information about the types of teacher-education programs of colleges or universities throughout the state and information concerning supply and demand of teachers at various grade levels and in various fields.

7. *Assignment of teachers by local boards.* The state education authorities should give top priority to the development of regulations insuring that a teacher will be assigned only to those teaching duties for which he is

specifically prepared, and should enforce these regulations rigorously.

10. *Certification reciprocity among states.* Whenever a teacher has been certified by one state under the provisions of Recommendations 1 and 2, his certificate should be accepted as valid in any other state.

GROUP B RECOMMENDATIONS INVOLVING APPRO-
PRIATIONS BY STATE LEGISLATURES

4. *State financial responsibility for practice teaching.* The state should provide financial assistance to local boards to insure high-quality practice teaching as part of the preparation of teachers enrolled in either private or public institutions.

12. *Loan policy for future teachers.* Each state should develop a loan policy for future teachers aimed at recruiting into the profession the most able students; the requirements for admission to the teacher-training institutions within the state should be left to the institution, but the state should set a standard for the recipients in terms of scholastic aptitude; the amount of the loan should be sufficient to cover expenses, and the loan should be cancelled after four or five years of teaching in the public schools of the state.

GROUP C RECOMMENDATIONS REQUIRING ACTION
BY A LOCAL SCHOOL BOARD, EITHER ACTING ALONE
OR IN CONJUNCTION WITH STATE ACTION

3. *Cooperating teachers in practice teaching.* Public school systems that enter contracts with a college

or university for practice teaching should designate, as classroom teachers working with practice teaching, only those persons in whose competence as teachers, leaders, and evaluators they have the highest confidence, and should give such persons encouragement by reducing their work loads and raising their salaries.

11. *Initial probationary period of employment.* During the initial probationary period, local school boards should take specific steps to provide the new teacher with every possible help in the form of: (a) limited teaching responsibility; (b) aid in gathering instructional materials; (c) advice of experienced teachers whose own load is reduced so that they can work with the new teacher in his own classroom; (d) shifting to more experienced teachers those pupils who create problems beyond the ability of the novice to handle effectively; and (e) specialized instruction concerning the characteristics of the community, the neighborhood, and the students he is likely to encounter.

23. *Revision of salary schedule by local boards.* School boards should drastically revise their salary schedule. There should be a large jump in salary when a teacher moves from the probationary status to tenure. Any salary increments based on advanced studies should not be tied to course credits earned (semester hours), but only to the earning of a master's degree, based normally on full-time residence or four summer sessions in which the program is directed toward the development of the competence of the teacher as a teacher. Such a salary increment should be made mandatory by state law.

24. *Financial assistance to teachers for study in summer schools.* School boards or the state should provide financial assistance so that teachers may attend

summer school after enrolling in a graduate school for the purpose of completing a program of the type stated in Recommendation 23.

25. *Leaves of absence for further education of teachers.* School boards should provide leave of absence with salary for a full-time semester residence at a university to enable teachers to study toward a master's program, provided this program is designed to increase the competence of the teacher; state funds should be available for this purpose.

27. *In-service education of teachers.* To insure that the teachers are up to date, particularly in a period of rapid change (as in mathematics and physics), a school board should contract with an educational institution to provide short-term seminars (often called workshops) during the school year so that *all* the teachers, without cost to them, may benefit from the instruction. Such seminars or workshops might also study the particular educational problems of a given school or school district. (No credit toward salary increases would be given.)

GROUP D RECOMMENDATIONS REQUIRING ACTION BY THE FACULTIES, ADMINISTRATIVE OFFICERS, AND TRUSTEES OF AN INSTITUTION ENGAGED IN EDUCATING TEACHERS FOR THE PUBLIC ELEMENTARY AND SECONDARY SCHOOLS

2. *Collegiate or university responsibility.* Each college or university should be permitted to develop in detail whatever program of teacher education it considers most desirable, subject only to two conditions: first, the president of the institution in behalf of the entire

faculty involved—academic as well as professional—certifies that the candidate is adequately prepared to teach on a specific level or in specific fields, and second, the institution establishes in conjunction with a public school system a state-approved practice-teaching arrangement.

13. *The all-university approach to teacher training.* If the institution is engaged in educating teachers, the lay board trustees should ask the faculty or faculties whether in fact there is a continuing and effective all-university (or interdepartmental) approach to the education of teachers; and if not, why not?

14. *Requirements for collegiate or university teacher-education programs.* The board of trustees should ask the faculty to justify the present requirements for a bachelor's degree *for future teachers* with particular reference to the breadth of the requirements and to spell out what in fact are the total educational exposures (school and college) demanded now in the fields of (a) mathematics, (b) physical science, (c) biological science, (d) social science, (e) English literature, (f) English composition, (g) history, (h) philosophy.

15. *Foreign language preparation.* If courses are required in a foreign language, evidence of the degree of mastery obtained by fulfilling the minimum requirement for a degree should be presented to the board of trustees.

16. *The establishment of "clinical professors."* The professor from the college or university who is to supervise and assess the practice teaching should have had much practical experience. His status should be analogous to that of a clinical professor in certain medical schools.

17. *Basic preparation of elementary teachers.* (a)

The program for teachers of kindergarten and grades 1, 2, and 3 should prepare them in the content and methodology of all subjects taught in these early school years. Depth in a single subject or cluster of subjects is not necessary. (b) The program for teachers of grades 4, 5, and 6 should provide depth of content and methods of teaching in a specific subject or cluster of subjects normally taught in these grades, with only an introduction to the remaining elementary school subjects.

18. *Practice teaching for elementary teachers*. All future elementary teachers should engage in practice teaching for a period of at least eight weeks, spending a minimum of three hours a day in the classroom; the period must include at least three weeks of full responsibility for the classroom under the direction of a cooperating teacher and the supervision of a clinical professor.

19. *Adequate staffing of small colleges training elementary teachers*. Those responsible for financing and administering small colleges should consider whether they can afford to maintain an adequate staff for the preparation of elementary school teachers. Unless they are able to employ the equivalent of three or four professors devoting their time to elementary education, they should cease attempting to prepare teachers for the elementary schools.

20. *Single-field diploma for secondary school teachers*. An institution should award a teaching certificate for teachers in grades 7 to 12 in one field only.

21. *Clinical professors in institutions educating secondary teachers*. Every institution awarding a special teaching certificate for secondary school teachers should have on the staff a clinical professor for each field or combination of closely related fields.

22. *Teaching diploma for art, music, and physical education teachers.* An institution offering programs in art or music or physical education should be prepared to award a teaching diploma in each of these fields without grade designation; institutional programs should not attempt to develop competency in more than one field in four years.

26. *Master's degree programs.* The graduate schools of education or their equivalent (in universities organized without such separate degree-granting schools) should devise a program for increasing the competence of teachers as teachers with the following characteristics: (1) It should be open to any graduate of the same institution in the same field of endeavor (e.g., elementary education, secondary school social studies, etc.). (2) Courses should be allowed for credit toward the 30 semester hours whether or not the courses are of an elementary nature, provided they are clearly courses needed to increase the competence of the teacher. (3) No credit toward the degree should be given for extension courses or courses taken on campus while the teacher is engaged on a full-time teaching job. (4) Passing of a comprehensive examination should be required for the master's degree, as is now the case in some institutions. (5) The summer-school sessions should be arranged so that four summer residences will complete the degree requirements, or two summers plus one full-time semester residence. (6) If the offering in the arts and sciences is not wide enough to provide meaningful work in the summer session (as it would not be in some state colleges), arrangements should be made for the transfer of credit from a university summer school with a good offering of courses in subjectmatter fields. (7) For elementary teachers, the degree should be master of

education in elementary education; for secondary teachers, master of education in English (or science, social science, modern languages, or mathematics).

Group e concerning voluntary accrediting agencies

8. *Composition of NCATE.* The governing boards of NCATE and the regional associations should be significantly broadened to give greater power to (a) representatives of scholarly disciplines in addition to professional education, and to (b) informed representatives of the lay public.

9. *Function of NCATE.* NCATE and the regional associations should serve only as advisory bodies to teacher-preparing institutions and local school boards. They should, on the request of institutions, send in teams to study and make recommendations concerning the whole or any portion of a teacher–education program. They should, on the request of local boards, evaluate employment policies. They should provide a forum in which issues concerning teacher education and employment are debated.

3

Dr. Conant
and His Critics

*Lindley J. Stiles**

The Education of American Teachers is about the politics of teacher education. Such a focus, understood by some reviewers ([Notes] 22, 23) and criticized by others, (15, 16, 37, 38, 39), was dictated by the subject treated. The preparation of elementary and secondary school teachers in the United States today is as much a matter of politics, both legal and professional, as it is education. Thus, under present conditions, to improve the way teachers are educated, one must deal in politics.

Dr. Conant set out to arbitrate the century-long battle between professors of education and those in the liberal arts. His aim was to point the way to joint efforts between the two groups to improve teacher education. Pursuit of this objective led him through the catacombs

* For information about Lindley J. Stiles, see Preface, p. vii.

of political controls and harassments which confront institutions that educate teachers. His central and most controversial recommendation was the result: Encourage college and university faculties to find better ways of preparing teachers by freeing teacher-education programs from externally imposed prescriptions and internal control by educationalists.

The proposal to emancipate teacher education from the political arena and to return it to its natural academic habitat threatens to fall like a *coup de grace* on current efforts to forestall a complete reorganization of the National Council for Accreditation of Teacher Education (NCATE). Dr. Conant's book and the subsequent discussion of it have raised to public view the basic issues that divide institutional faculties and generally negate efforts to strengthen teacher education. The initial impact of *The Education of American Teachers* can be estimated from the early responses of the critics and the actions taken within the states. It is possible to make a preliminary analysis of these reactions. Also, perhaps the time has come to examine more closely the basic assumptions that underlie the book's recommendations.

CONANT'S CREDENTIALS

Dr. Conant is no outsider to teacher education. He has, in fact, undergone a long, self-imposed apprenticeship in preparation for this study. Contrary to the impression given by some critics (30), Dr. Conant's interest began when, as a young president of Harvard, he realized that he might make a useful contribution to strengthening elementary and secondary schools. For a quarter of a century, he had read copiously, plagued his educator friends with questions, attended educational meetings, and accepted assignments on national professional bodies, including the Educational Policies Commission of the National Education Association (1941–1963)—all in an effort to educate himself about education.

By 1952, he was already deeply engrossed in improving teacher education. In his Page Barbour Lectures at the University of Virginia that year, he admonished liberal arts professors to "stop wringing their hands" about the state of teacher education. Instead, he urged them to join with professors of education to bring about improvements. He examined the role of teacher education in his own university and established a new type of graduate school of education.

His list of published books in the field of education compares favorably with the production of the most prolific professors of education in quantity, range of subjects, and quality. In fact, Dr. Conant is fully qualified by both scholarship and experience to hold a post as professor or dean in a school of education in the best universities in the country. His only deficiency would be a paper one: His academic transcript would not show a specified number of credits in education courses.

With most critics, Dr. Conant's qualification for dealing with the problems of teacher education stands unquestioned. Titles they confer upon him include "one of our most prominent educators" (38, 39), "the Winston Churchill of American education" (32), "education's most eminent elder statesman" (26). Whatever the title, he is truly a man with a mission—to strengthen American education.

To this mission, the author of *The Education of*

American Teachers brings three unique qualities: He possesses a deep understanding of and an unqualified dedication to what he calls the "democratic-social component." Progress in our society is achieved only by dealing skillfully and diplomatically with the competing forces that struggle to dominate all. Dr. Conant is willing to walk the way of democracy on the road to its improvement. Second is his ability to give to facts and opinions a perception that clarifies their meaning. Few are as skilled in understanding the views and values of people; few can cut through sham and subterfuge with so much ease; few can hold for balanced and objective scrutiny so many competing practices. Finally, Dr. Conant is a diplomat. He deals in the politics of the possible. His role is one of negotiation; his goal is to find the highest level of compromise by which all are willing to live. This was the purpose of his book.

INITIAL IMPACT

Perhaps no recent book on education has enjoyed the initial reception accorded this one. Its sales exceeded 50,000 copies within three months (13), and it continues on many best-seller lists. It was chosen as a Book-of-the-Month Club alternate selection. Within a month after publication, radio and television networks had featured it, and newspapers and popular as well as professional journals, reportedly over 1,200, had rushed into print with extensive reviews.

In a taped interview released in October, Dr. Conant said, "The most important objective in my book would be a vigorous national debate among educators and laymen on the question of how to educate the teachers of our youth." This hope promises to be realized. Lay organizations, like the League of Women Voters, Parents-and-Teachers Associations, civic and luncheon clubs, are devoting meetings to teacher education. Professional associations are centering their attention on the criticisms and recommendations advanced. Members of Dr. Conant's staff, as well as other leaders in teacher education, find it difficult to keep up with invitations to speak to interested groups. The American Association of Colleges for Teacher Education brought Dr. Conant back from West Berlin to speak to its national convention in February. While in the United States, he was swamped with requests for speaking and interview engagements. Unlike previous criticisms of teacher education (21, 35) that were ignored by the professionals and unread by the public, this book seems destined to get a hearing.

Some indication of the extent and nature of this hearing can also be gathered from the responses of 38 chief state school officers to a letter requesting a description of any action their state is taking on the Conant recommendations. Most state officers agreed with the commissioner who wrote, "In general, it has stimulated new interest in examining every aspect of our operation." At least two states, New York and Wisconsin, have initiated major efforts to test certain of the recommendations, and several others have financed studies on a less ambitious scale. There is, however, a tendency in some states to concur with the statement that,

. . . it would be presumptuous to expect a publication of this kind to have much of an impact immediately. . . . On many points we feel that we are up to and even far in advance of the recommendations made by Dr. Conant. On some other points there is very little likelihood that the recommendations will be given any kind of favorable consideration.

DEBATE BREWING

Reactions to *The Education of American Teachers* forecast the debate that Dr. Conant hoped to inspire (39). They ranged from "nothing less than insurrectionary" (22), "he calls for radical change" (13, 18), "recommendations for the revolution" (30), and "a drastic departure from present practices" (11), to such opposite responses as "it has all been said before" (27), "book is unoriginal" (26), and "reform envisioned is an essentially conservative one" (23).

One reaction was to criticize Dr. Conant for not writing a different book or for not treating particular topics close to the reviewer's interest (1, 2, 4). These are typical: "In short, one of the things Dr. Conant should have been considering all along was what kind of people become teachers . . ." (15); "avoidance of all substantive questions in the political, social, or economic problems of education and American culture" (28); "Conant does not deal with some major problems of teacher education today" (19); "Dr. Conant's complete lack of reference to the curriculum materials developments and therefore to their potential influences on teacher education is provocative indeed" (17); "study does not provide any historical prospective in teacher education" (10); "Conant misses the point in what needs to be remedied . . . The heart of the matter is in the development of a 'content' of education for teachers" (1).

Few of the reviews that have appeared to date deal with the book as a whole. Some have been only informative (4, 19, 25, 34, 41). Only Spaulding (33) and Anderson *et al.* (1), reacted to all 27 of Conant's recommendations. Other more comprehensive treatments include those by Robb (30), Koerner (22), Chandler (6), Ladd (11), Broudy (5), and Hechinger (18). The certification requirements recommendation (No. 1 in the summary, p. 210) is the only one mentioned in almost all of the 40 selected reviews. Other points dealt with extensively are the establishment of the clinical professorship, certification reciprocity among states, revision of salary schedules by local boards, and the function and composition of NCATE.

The recommended changes in certification policy and the proposed reduction of NCATE to advisory status are the points that capture the concern of professional educationalists. Reviewers in this category who favored Dr. Conant's proposals were Chandler (6), Spaulding (33), (with the exception of part "b" in certification), Woodring (41), and Keeton (20). Those opposed included Robb (30), Maucher (24), Stratemeyer (37), Rosebrock (31), the Deans of the School of Education of New York University (1), and Stinnett (36). Noneducationalist reviewers who expressed reactions on these points—Koerner, Friedenberg, Taylor, and Hechinger for example—were generally in agreement with the proposals.

On NCATE

Koerner's analysis of the NCATE recommendation is perhaps the most penetrating: Conant "proposes a sort of *coup d'etat* in the political structure of teacher education and sweeping decentralization of power . . . Happily, he characterizes NCATE for what it is: a quasi-legal body of tremendous national power that relies for state acceptance on the political power of the NEA, and is neither voluntary nor independent . . . His intent is admirable, but his recommendation is wide of the mark. How will teacher education be free of NCATE domination by making the agency 'advisory'? We all know that NCATE's brand of voluntarism is laced with Orwellian irony: what is voluntary is coercive; freedom is slavery" (22). A typical defense of NCATE is this one: "Conant's statement that TEPS and NCATE seek control through detailed prescription is of doubtful accuracy. . . . A more realistic and useful purpose would be served by recommendations found wanting in the present writing which would improve the present NCATE program" (37). Maucher, an NCATE Council member, in a praise-God-for-Conant type of review, ultimately seems to reject all of Dr. Conant's proposals (as probably many other educationalists do) on the sole basis of the accreditation issue: "Mr. Conant's recommendations are interdependent, as he himself says. There must be a high degree of selectivity (a rejection, if you please, of many students, fees in hand, who want to prepare to teach); faculties must be carefully chosen; old status patterns broken; state department staffs retooled perhaps. Without the force of accreditation, I don't see these things being done widely and in sufficient degree. And, if it served in an *advisory* capacity only, I would state categorically that an NCATE, or any other national professional accrediting body, would die" (24).

In trying to counteract Conant on NCATE, some educationalists argue that individual states and institutions—others, not their own—cannot be trusted to maintain high standards. A national accrediting agency is required, therefore, to impose quality from without (12, 24, 25, 30, 31, 34).

Toward basic assumptions

Certain critics fear that Conant's personal prominence rather than the intrinsic value of his ideas will gain acceptance for his recommendations (5, 10). Some, however, appreciate the support his prestige lends to opening the problems of teacher education to general debate (6, 22, 28, 29, 32, 35). A distressing number of reviews, many by professional educators who should be thinking most carefully about the book, contain distortions of meaning. For example, "Apparently Dr. Conant has concluded that a shift in the power structure giving control to the academicians is the only hope for the changes that the college-oriented academic groups consider desirable" (31). Dr. Conant actually recommended an approach to teacher training in which *all* professors concerned with preparing teachers cooperate in making decisions. Another common misinterpretation is that "Conant would abolish all education courses except student teaching" (12). This, as Pomeroy points out, is simply not true (28).

One misses from many of the reviews a penetration beyond the recommendations made. Lacking is a search for the basic assumptions which underlie the proposals for action. Those who agree with the author tend to applaud him as a careful, analytical scholar, whereas others who disagree argue dogmatically against objectionable proposals.

Since the book's publication, Dr. Conant and members of his research staff have sought to make clear the assumptions which underlie their recommendations (3, 9). These may be summarized as follows (3):

1. Beyond highly abstract generalizations, no statement can be made which describes teacher education in the nation, within a given state, or sometimes even on a specific campus.

2. The most significant decisions concerning teacher education have always been and will continue to be made on particular college campuses. These include (a) selection of faculty, (b) content emphasis and presentation of material in courses, and (c) evaluation of student performance.

3. Each campus and state must make decisions in terms of its distinctive traditions and consistent with its characteristic political ethos.

4. Beyond student teaching or the clinical experience, which everyone grants is important, there is no national consensus concerning any element of teacher education, nor is there sufficient evidence to warrant one.

5. The major challenge facing those concerned with teacher education is working out the political processes by which the present array of groups seeking to influence it can express their legitimate interests.

6. Decisions about teacher-education curricula should be made by the teaching faculties on specific campuses, but subject to two conditions: that they be based on careful study of conditions in public schools, and that public school authorities and state officials have the opportunity to bring about changes should they discover specific weaknesses in the teachers produced by a particular college.

7. Within the professional curriculum it is highly probable that effective instruction can come only from intermediary professors who bring to bear on educational problems such well established disciplines as history, psychology, and philosophy, and clinical professors who bring to bear on teacher preparation extensive continuing and intellectually examined classroom experience.

REALISM OF VISION

Based on such assumptions, Dr. Conant's recommendations assume a character of genuine realism. Recognizing that in the final analysis the college or university faculty determines the quality of teachers prepared, he proposes to allow them freedom and to assign them responsibility cooperatively to improve their products. Dr. Conant and his associates realized what many engaged in teacher education already knew: Licensing and accrediting processes operate more as harassments than as controls. What they had done is to call attention to the sheer impossibility of controlling the quality of teachers through controlling certification or accrediting procedures or by an interlocking of the two processes as 28 states are now attempting. He made it clear, in his book and while speaking to the American Association of Colleges for Teacher Education, that the use of accreditation as a stamp of quality is a sham. His words in Chicago were, "Anyone who has visited a great many NCATE-accredited institutions must know that some are excellent. Others are of such quality that a state department must be either uninformed or irresponsible to recommend the automatic certification of all their graduates" (9).

The real strength behind state licensing and national accrediting operations, Dr. Conant realizes, has been the determination of deans and professors of education to maintain control of teacher education. Unwilling to permit their courses to compete on the open market, such professors have turned to state departments and the national accrediting agency for protection of their vested interests—all under the guise of "professionalization of teaching." On the grounds that liberal arts professors were uninterested and insufficiently oriented to schools to decide the liberal education and special preparation needed by prospective teachers, many schools of education have relied upon the outside political power of the profession to keep such decisions in their control. Thus, Dr. Conant properly asserts the all-institution approach as the means by which to achieve one of his prime objectives: a true sharing of power between professors of education and those in the liberal arts.

Clearly, Conant has issued the sharpest challenge to teacher education since the creation of the normal school. Significantly, he points in the opposite direction. His recommendations come into an atmosphere of tension and controversy created by a revolution that was already underway. Were he to fire his salvos and then retire, it is doubtful that any long-range gains would be achieved. Such, however, is not the Conant pattern. Already he has returned once from West Germany to follow up his book with analyses and discussions with leaders in teacher education. If, as seems likely, the establishment proves too complex or inflexible to make changes, it is highly probable that Dr. Conant will carry his fight to the lay public, where his ideas already enjoy considerable support. His behavior indicates that he has joined the revolution. His entry may well supply the additional moral force and intellectual vigor required for victory.

Notes

1. Anderson, W., Griffiths, D. E., Payne, J. C., Beaman, Florence, & Fields, M. R. *Reactions to the book by James B. Conant*. New York: New York Univer. School of Educ., 1963 (mimeo).
2. Beck, R. H. Review. *J. Teach, Educ.*, 1964, *15*, 37–40.
3. Borrowman, M. L. Conant's recommendations concerning teacher education. Address to the Association of State Universities and Land-Grant Colleges, Chicago, Ill., 12 November, 1963.
4. Boutwell, W. D. Review. *PTA Mag.*, 1963, *58*, 14–15.
5. Broudy, H. S. *Conant on the education of teachers*. Unpubl. MS., 1963.
6. Chandler, B. J. The Conant report and Illinois. *Chicago Sunday Sun-Times*, 13 October, 1963, Sec. 2, 1–3.
7. Chase, F. S. Does the Conant plan actually go far enough? *Chicago Sunday Sun-Times*, 13 October, 1963, Sec. 2, 3.
8. Conant, J. B. *The education of American teachers*. New York: McGraw-Hill, 1963.
9. Conant, J. B. The certification of teachers: the restricted state-approved program approach. Fifth Charles W. Hunt Lecture, delivered to the Association of Colleges for Teacher Education, Chicago, Ill., 19 February, 1964.
10. Edelfelt, R. A. What do you think of the Conant report? *J. Teach. Educ.*, 1963, *14*, 359–361.
11. *Education Digest*, 1963, *29*, 62.
12. English, W. F. Review. *Coll. & Univer.*, 1964, *39*, 217–220.

13. Footlick, J. K. Teacher training sharply attacked; changes to come. *National Observer*, 13 January, 1964, 1, 16.

14. Freedman, N. Review. *J. Teach. Educ.*, 1964, *15*, 29–31.

15. Friedenberg, E. Z. Lower-middle classroom. *New York Rev. Books*, 1963, *1*, 20–21.

16. Gideonse, H. Comments on the Conant report. Unpubl. MS., 1963.

17. Grennan, Sister Jacqueline. Review. *J. Teach. Educ.*, 1964, *15*, 23–25.

18. Hechinger, F. M. Dr. Conant's bombshell. *Reporter*, 1963, *29*, 44–46.

19. Hodenfield, G. K. Dr. Conant proposes: Loans to train teachers. *Philadelphia Inquirer*, 15 September, 1963.

20. Keeton, M. Review. *J. Teach. Educ.*, 1964, *15*, 7–11.

21. Koerner, J. D. *The miseducation of American teachers*. Boston: Houghton Mifflin, 1963.

22. Koerner, J. D. Proposals for radical reform *Phi Delta Kappan*, 1963, *45*, 7–10.

23. Ladd, E. T. Review. *Harvard Educ. Rev.*, 1964, *34*, 91–96.

24. Maucker, J. W. Review. *J. Teach. Educ.*, 1964, *15*, 2–6.

25. Michalak, J. Review. *New York Herald Tribune*, 24 November, 1963, 20.

26. Newsweek, 21 September, 1963, 9.

27. Parsons, Cynthia. *Christian Science Monitor*, 16 September, 1963, 1.

28. Pomeroy, E. C. Review. *J. Teach. Educ.*, 1964, *15*, 20–22.

29. Purcell, B. R. Quoted by *National Observer*, 13 January, 1964, 16.

30. Robb, F. C. The academic preparation of teachers: Conant's proposals. *Sci.*, 1963, *141*, 1166–1168.

31. Rosebrock, A. F. Review. *J. Teach. Educ.*, 1964, *15*, 12–19.

32. Sizer, T. R. Review. *Focus*, 1963, *14*, 1–4.
33. Spaulding, W. B. Teacher education. *J. Teach. Educ.*, 1963, *14*, 456–461.
34. Stein, J. W. Review. *Library J.*, 1963, 88, 3610.
35. Stiles, L. J., Barr, A. S., Douglass, H. R., & Mills, H. H. *Education in the United States*. New York: Ronald Press, 1960.
36. Stinnett, T. M. Review. *J. Teach. Educ.*, 1964, *15*, 41–45.
37. Stratemeyer, Florence, Review. *NEA J.*, 1963, *52*, 64, 70.
38. Taylor, H. New blood, not dry words. *Washington Post (Book Week)*, 15 September, 1963, 1, 32.
39. *Time.* 27 September, 1963, 55–56.
40. Whittier, C. T. Review. *J. Teach. Educ.*, 1964, *15*, 26–28.
41. Woodring, P. Conant's report on teacher education. *Sat. Rev.*, 1963, 46, 49–51.

4

Future Implications and Repercussions of the Report

Harold Taylor[*]

Let me begin by stating again the central theme of Dr. Conant's book, and describing the universe of discourse the book inhabits.

The crucial issue in the education of American teachers, says the book, is a quarrel between the academics and the professional educators over how teachers should be certified, and who should certify them. This is what the book is about. This is what Dr. Conant again told us last night in more explicit detail—how to settle the quarrel and how to certify teachers properly. The rest of the book's arguments and issues stem from this central theme.

My trouble with the book and with Dr. Conant's theme is, therefore, almost total. I do not think this is

[*] For information about Harold Taylor, see Preface, p. xi.

all the crucial issue in the education of teachers, and the universe of discourse which the book inhabits is not the one, in my judgment, in which most of the serious problems in education now exist.

The accreditation problem is, of course, important. It is, of course, true, as Dr. Conant says, that the present certification is bankrupt in many states. The system does not guarantee the development of good teachers. Nor can it do so. It should be changed, and as quickly as possible. I agree with Dr. Conant—the responsibility for certifying teachers should be put squarely up to the colleges and universities.

However, to treat as important a subject as the education of teachers solely within the narrow environment of matters having to do with the academies and their bureaucracies and the readjustment of the agencies, requirements, courses and credits, is to define education itself as an administrative means for transmitting knowledge and certifying academic achievement.

The importance which has been attached by the public and by educators to these secondary matters raised by Dr. Conant, by reason of their selection in the book as the crucial questions for settlement, has distracted both educators and the public from the real issues which must be faced if the American educational system is to do what the society is crying out for it to do. One immediate effect of the book, as far as my personal experience with educators around the country is concerned, has been to reduce almost every discussion of matters in the training of teachers to jurisdictional disputes and tedious debates over credit and course requirements.

I find that it is almost impossible to persuade people to change the subject once they get started on certification requirements. I refer to a phrase from the philosopher F. H. Bradley, in his reference to Hegel. It seems to me that what we have here is, "a ballet of the bloodless categories."

The educational philosophy now dominant in the public mind and among the majority of educators is not one of concern for the liberation of talent within the student. The direction of educational thinking over these past ten to fifteen years has been conservative, restrictive and, it seems to me, inhibiting. In terms of public policy and public statements about public policy, education is most often linked with an international competition in military, economic and political affairs. Education is considered, by and large, to be an instrument for developing increased technological and logistical strength in international competition, especially with the Russians.

The idea of searching for talent and educating it for the technological, the scientific and the academic skills, the incessant testing, the scholastic awards for high achievement, the special programs for the gifted, the advanced placement for special students, these are all devices for meeting certain of the country's educational and social needs. But they do not do so in order to build a new and enriching social order. They do so in order to staff the manpower needs of the present industrial and cultural establishment. The changes in educational practice which are talked about consist mainly of large mechanical and structural arrangements of the kind to which Dr. Conant devotes so much of his attention in the present book.

What disturbs me about Dr. Conant's range of recommendations is that they provide for the transmission of American, white, middle-class Protestant, Western culture, without questioning whether the values of this culture are worth transmitting in their present form. In the cycle of teaching development, high school students who pass courses in American history, English and American literature, science, mathematics and a European language, go on to teacher preparation institutions where they study mainly the same subjects for another four years. Along with this goes practical experience of teaching children brought up within the same culture, and at no point, as far as I can see, is there any opportunity for breaking the cycle and re-examining the culture. It is a process of adaptation, not of re-creation.

In other sectors of public discussion, one finds great interest in the use of television for handling large classes, the development of standard curricula which can be handled by standard and replaceable faculty members, the consolidation of smaller schools into big ones, the shifting of college curricular material into the high school, the construction of new buildings and classrooms, and so on. But through the whole of the discussion runs the central theme that education consists of the achievement of academic grades, the acquirement of academic credit, the taking of academic tests, and the acquisition of various certificates.

In the process, the old-fashioned ideal of the progressives, that education must confront directly the moral, political and social questions of the going social order, has been lost in the welter of mechanical detail.

I believe that the purpose of education is to make people sensitive to the conditions of their own existence, and to the situation of man in the world. The study of physics, for example, is the way in which one becomes aware of nature. Physics is a language which describes something which otherwise could not be understood by humanity at large. In this it is no different than poetry or the theatre. These, too, are ways of becoming sensitive to existence and to the situation of man.

When we think in this larger context and wish to move beyond the limits of academic discussion, we find that Dr. Conant's book affirms and strengthens the present academic structure in its most conservative tendencies. The book already has assumed the status of a public document. It has had, and will continue to have, a wide influence. That influence will be to restrict the area of debate among educators to matters lying outside the going concerns and needs of society. Whenever those issues are injected into public discussions of education, they will come from sources other than this book.

In fact, I have been longing to find a book on education which simply started with the idea that the way to save the country and strengthen it beyond belief is to have everyone from kindergarten to the end of college study the creative arts, philosophy, and the nature of society, on the grounds that theatre, dance, music, painting, sculpture, poetry and philosophy are more important than anything else in learning to understand and re-create human life. These, therefore, are the things which should be central to the curriculum. We could allow a certain amount of science, mathematics, engineering, law and other things of that sort. These could be added as electives if there were any time, since as far as understanding oneself and one's place in society, they are frills.

If we really wish to make this country strong and want to show the world what we are and what we can do through reforming our curriculum, why don't we educate a new generation of poets, historians and artists, some of whom could also handle the sciences? That would baffle the Russians and take their minds off the nuclear threat.

In fact, when we look at the structure of a given society, to take two societies at random presently in the news, the United States and the Soviet Union, we find that the most powerful elements in these societies for shaping the future are not the academic curricula experts, not the technologists, the engineers or even the scientists, but the poets, the writers and the critics. In the Soviet Union, the inner force which is now loosening up the conception of what a true Soviet society should be, is not to be found in the scientific and technological and academic personnel. Those people are doing pretty much what they are told to do and what the curriculum demands. The developing social forces are to be found among the poets, writers and painters who are now speaking to the Soviet people about the individual truths which they have found, and who speak of human consciousness and the need for it to expand, the need to breathe pure air. Pasternak is the one to worry about; Yevtushenko, not Gagarin or Titov or any of the astronauts or the Soviet educators.

It seems to me that we must look at the real educational question and ask ourselves, "Who creates the images of life which we then pursue in the accomplishment of personal and social values for the American community and for the world community at large?" When we think of the curriculum in these terms, we cannot simply say that the education of the elementary school teacher or the high school teacher is complete if we can certify that the high school or elementary school teacher is skilled in teaching a subject and can be certified as one who has taken four years of the regular academic course in the high school and four years of regular academic courses in college. This is a conception of education which betrays the true purpose of learning.

In this connection, I cannot avoid the responsibility of commenting, however briefly, on Dr. Conant's book as a written work. As a literary document, the book will scarcely live and promises little for future literary critics and literary historians, if that is a matter of interest. The style is middle twentieth century, academic committee prose of the kind found in government documents, the manuals of college outline series and committee curriculum reports.

I assure you I say this without intended malice, but merely in descriptive terms, since the approach Dr. Conant has deliberately chosen is, in his words, that of advisor to an all-university committee, and it is in the committee style of thought that the book is conceived. The style, however, does reflect the thought and as in all other written documents, literary or otherwise, the style at a given point becomes the thought. The process by which Dr. Conant assumes education can reform itself is by way of all-university committees of representatives from professional education and the academic faculties.

Although in the present book, and again in his lecture last night, Dr. Conant is against political horse trading in the State Legislature by which, for example, credits in chemistry can be exchanged for credits in education; in fact, the recommended method of bringing about changes in the curriculum of teacher preparation is by the committee system. I must confess to a dislike amounting almost to armed violence for exclusive reliance on committees, mainly because the operations of university committees have now become standardized bureaucratic means of choking off most private, creative thought about education. The reason is simple. Not only are the committees chosen or elected with an eye to the proper representation of the various vested interests in academic subject matter, budget and size of departments, but the method of thought rests on the fallacious notion that once a consensus has been reached on any human question, the question itself has been settled satisfactorily.

To put it another way, once the committee's members have voted for the inclusion of required courses for a degree or certificate, their conclusions are reported unanimously as what everyone has had to agree to for one reason or another. This means that since the result is what everybody thinks will be accepted by everybody, it is often what nobody thinks about anything.

As an approach to educational change, it accepts the entire cultural context on which the academic high school is based and the standard academic program which goes with it. I was astonished to find Dr. Conant referring to himself in last night's lecture as a revolutionary. This is not the word I would use to describe the author of the ideas in this report.

On the other hand, there are two important matters which Dr. Conant's book settles, I hope for all time. The first is that the difference between the amount of regulation liberal arts courses required by the liberal arts colleges and teachers' colleges is nonexistent. By reference to the requirement lists of typical institutions of both kinds, Dr. Conant disposes of that fallacy. What he does not do is to dispose of the fallacy that by taking these courses the students in either kind of institution become liberally educated.

The second matter is that all a teacher needs to have

by way of preparation to teach is a set of required classroom courses in the academic curriculum. Dr. Conant's recommendation for practice teaching and allied seminars is crucially important for correcting the false notion that sheer exposure to classroom courses is preparation enough for a career in teaching. What Dr. Conant does not recognize is that technical training in practice teaching is still not enough. What is needed is direct experience with the reality of political, social and moral issues within the society itself.

We need to look again at the problem of curriculum in terms of where the serious purpose of the teacher is to be found, the way in which his life can be placed in the service of the creation of new knowledge, and the efforts to make the young more sensitive to the conditions of their own lives. On this matter the report brings us very little.

The comments on the elementary school teacher curriculum do admit that psychology is a subject worth studying, particularly if in psychology one considers those aspects of the discipline which can help to predict human behavior. This seems to me to be the least interesting part of psychology and the least important aspect for the education of teachers.

In his preface to *Endymion,* Keats says:

The imagination of a boy is healthy and the mature imagination of a man is healthy, but there is the space of life between in which the soul is in ferment, the character undecided, the way of life uncertain, the ambition thicksighted.

An educational system which took account of what Keats has said would invent ways in which the young, from the ages of eleven, twelve and thirteen, could move toward their full development in the stress and strain of later adolescence. This is the space of life in which the soul is in ferment, the character undecided, the way of life uncertain and the ambition thick-sighted. Each of us forgets very quickly the experiences which affect us in that space of life, and no teacher is able to understand the needs of the child in school unless his memory and consciousness are constantly refreshed and informed by a knowledge of the psychology of the young. That is a major purpose of studying psychology as a preparation for teaching.

If one is to teach in order to reach those sensitive areas of human consciousness where all important matters rest, there must be more than scholastic exercise in an academic program which puts in the place of state-certification requirements merely those requirements set down by an academic faculty. It is vain to hope that by doing so, a young person who has come to a college where teachers are prepared, is going to be able to extend the range of his own sensitivity, his own awareness of himself, and, through his own intellectual initiative, become farsighted about the place of the teacher in his society or the place of man in the universe.

To think of matters of this kind as matters exclusively concerned with academic curricula is to misconstrue the problem of preparing teachers to teach. To dismiss, as Dr. Conant does, the need for self-understanding by suggesting that an academic course in psychology might be desirable is, in my judgment, a superficial approach to the real problems of education.

I would like to suggest for your attention an alternative to what amounts to a standard curriculum for elementary school and high school teachers. Dr. Conant recommends the study of the regular "hard" academic

subjects, and holds that courses in philosophy are un-
likely to be valuable unless taught by a regular academic
philosopher. I can think of no faster way to an intellectual stalemate than to study academic philosophy with
many of the academic philosophers now inhabiting the
universities.

If we wish to relate the life of the student to the
intellectual concerns of the teacher, we need to help the
student to find an image of himself and of what it
means to be a teacher in the full meaning of that term.

There is a good deal of talk in academic circles of
the situation of the college and of the importance of the
professor and the teacher in American society. But we
are not as accustomed as we should be to the fact that
the role of the teacher is rather like that of the artist,
and that to think of oneself as a teacher is one of the
ways in which the young can begin to occupy a new
world of their own creating.

It is not simply a question of professional recognition or status in the community, or status in the society,
or rank in the bureaucracy, or the ability to move upward to a higher level in the total organization of society. It is a conception of how one can think of oneself
as a certain kind of person. The poet becomes a certain
kind of person by thinking of himself as a poet. He then
takes daily action to become the kind of person he
wishes himself to be, after having first identified himself
as a poet.

We think our way into becoming a teacher by first
asserting to ourselves the fact that we wish to be. Then
we are impelled to move into those areas of knowledge
which can equip us to become the kind of person we
need to become in order to be a teacher. This sense of
vocation is crucial to the education of the teacher, and

one cannot feel a sense of vocation unless one has an image of oneself as a member of a community of scholars and intellectuals. One wishes, in this same way, to become a doctor, a poet, a composer, an architect. The teacher, on his part, must justify the assertion of himself as a teacher. Let me be quite specific.

I wish to suggest some alternative to the conceptions contained in Dr. Conant's book of what education can be and should be. We have had experiments over the years at Sarah Lawrence College in the achievement of that kind of selfhood which can come when one deliberately chooses to become what one may be by choosing the courses which one may study. It is not only a matter of choosing the courses, but of choosing the persons with whom one wishes to work, of choosing to be one kind of person rather than another.

Our Sarah Lawrence experiments in the education of teachers indicate that the student whose direct experience with children, either in the college nursery school, in a slum area, or in the middle-class areas of Yonkers, Mount Vernon or New York, gained from that experience a deep sense of need for more knowledge about education, about the social structure, about human nature, and about the subject matter of the curriculum. One of the most important contributions which Dr. Conant has made, through his book, is to describe in detail the crucial role of practical teaching experience in the preparation of the teacher. I am in great sympathy with Dr. Conant's notion that the evaluation of the teacher is to be achieved through a knowledge of how he teaches with his own students in his own classroom.

But I am out of sympathy with Dr. Conant's idea that the way to achieve mastery of a body of ideas and to achieve that deep ranging quality possessed by a good mind is by moving through the standard academic programs.

My own experience with students who are preparing to become teachers has led me to believe that students should be allowed to work in depth at the subjects in which they are interested. As they learn to live with children, to know them and to teach them, the body of subject matter the student-teacher is acquiring in college begins to take on new meaning. Teaching then becomes a matter of finding ways of sharing one's own knowledge and intellectual interests with the children. This is to say that the personal development of the student who is becoming a teacher should be the primary concern, and that experience in teaching and living with children is not merely professional training, but is part of the process of personal development. Such a development, in its intellectual dimension, is not possible unless the student is seriously interested in ideas and has a chance to become seriously involved in building a body of knowledge of his own making. We want teachers who study in order to know, because they *want* to know, not merely because they *have* to know in order to teach. Our experiments in teacher-preparation at Sarah Lawrence College, with an open choice rather than a required curriculum, support strongly the importance of individual choice in the liberal arts curriculum.

Flexibility of this kind is necessary in building the academic curriculum for teachers. We should not make separate arrangements for a standard catch-all academic program on the one hand, and a practice teaching program on the other. When we do so we reduce practice teaching to a means of acquiring a technique for transmitting the standard curriculum.

Let me be quite specific. I have been talking these last few weeks with some of the students who have organized tutorial projects for Negro children in the slums and others who have left college to go South to work on tutorial programs sponsored by the Student Non–Violent Coordinating Committee. These young people have been moved by a genuine feeling for the vocation of the teacher—they want to rescue the children from their ignorance, they want to help in raising the intellectual and the aesthetic level of children whose cultural and social deprivation has made it impossible for them to learn the academic subjects.

The vocation of the teacher has drawn these college students into communities which formerly had remained alien to them. Having gone to the slums to teach algebra or English, they have been inducted directly into the going concerns of their society. Having begun to teach algebra to the children, they have found that many of the problems which their eight, ten and twelve-year-old students are suffering from have no solutions aside from a drastic rearrangement of the economic, political and social order in which they exist. Through the route of algebra these students have widened their sense of vocation, and have then gone to the schools of education and to scholars who have more knowledge than they do, in order to find out how to deal with remedial reading problems, to discover more about the nature of American society and how to change that society in ways which can make some of these problems disappear. Through teaching algebra, they have learned about rent strikes and school boycotts, and the underlying causes and effects of poverty.

It is this relation of teaching to one's sense of mission, and to one's own body of knowledge which leads me to say that the way to build a new curriculum for the development of the American teacher is to free him to move into those areas of knowledge where he can indulge himself in a love of learning. Everything must be done to make it possible for him to learn the thing he wants to learn at the time he wants to learn it.

We do not need to have in the curriculum of elementary school teachers a standard body of required courses in order to make sure to ourselves, or to anyone else, that we have certified an elementary school teacher. The person who is on fire with an interest in American history is much more capable of teaching both American history and other subjects in social science if he has been allowed to enter deeply into the experience of historical study, conceived as the study of events in the human process, than he is by taking the sets of required courses now dominant in the American colleges, whether for teacher preparation, for preparation to enter graduate school, or even to graduate from college itself.

We are bound to move toward intellectual superficiality by the kind of curricular recommendations contained in Dr. Conant's report, and if there were more time I would be glad to develop in some detail the reasons why I believe this to be true. I wish I had time, also, to go through the list of questions in the opinionaire distributed to you, and to discuss each one of them with you. For example, one might comment on Item 15, "If a state is faced with a shortage of teachers, it would be far better to push the new developments (programmed instruction, team teaching, television, audio-visual techniques, et cetera) with the hope of decreasing the demand, than to continue to recruit teachers with very low intellectual ability."

There are a lot of questions begged in that statement. It is, of course, an impossible question to answer on an opinionaire or questionnaire or anything else of this kind. It refers to "very low intellectual ability." What is very low intellectual ability? Some of the lowest kinds of intellectual ability are to be found in some of the highest quality colleges. For example, there is a form of animal cunning which enables some students to do well on tests and which I would define as low intellectual ability. I find in Dr. Conant's report that the real questions about education and human life are constantly being begged by the assumption that education can be defined as academic, that intellectual ability is a matter of testable sets of attributes.

Or consider Item 26. "A good program for the preparation of teachers would be too difficult for students whose intellectual ability places them much below the top 30 percent in terms of the high school graduating class on a national basis."

Intellectual ability is not being measured in our present high schools in such a way that the choice of a top 30 percent by the standards we now apply would make a significant different in the choice of the best candidates for teaching. There are young people at the age of fifteen and sixteen in Mississippi at this moment who have had the equivalent of a fifth and sixth-grade education and who are out in the field teaching. They are teaching without benefit of formal preparation or of any tests now being applied for a top 30 percent. These are young people who are teachers and who can grow up to be teachers. They will form the indigenous leadership in Mississippi where just now the State is encapsulated in a quasi-fascist philosophy which does not allow the quality of teaching the Negroes in the State should have. Teaching is being done by unprepared people who, by tests, would be classed as ignorant. They are teachers. They will become better teachers. They will seek out the knowledge they need in order to bring out a resolution of the problems of their own society. But they do not fall into the magic percentages.

In the recruitment of candidates for teacher preparation it is wise to look not only for those who show talent for the "hard subjects." There are many intelligent young people who can and will learn what they need to know in order to teach "hard subjects" if they are themselves taught well by those who teach them. I would prefer to have experimental programs of the kind organized in the Freedom Schools now being developed by young people who have not graduated from high school, than I would to build a curriculum with the academic apparatus recommended in Dr. Conant's book.

I do not want to close without expressing appreciation for the amount of thought and effort which have gone into the report. The report contains facts and recommendations which should be gathered together in one place. What I am questioning is the value of this way of thinking about education. What I am advocating is the necessity of moving out of so narrow a framework of thought into the really deep, moral, social, political and philosophical questions which education must confront if it is to do anything significant for the American teacher and his students.

5

NSCTE Leaders Discuss Dr. Conant's Views

Edited by Robert M. Weiss[*]

DR. BRUBACHER: The panel agreed at lunch that most criticisms of Dr. Conant's latest book have concerned teacher certification. We decided to focus on the teaching of educational theory, a subject about which very little has been said, and on which Conant took a dim view yesterday and when he wrote his book.

DR. WAYLAND: "Theory" may understate the scope of our concern since "policy" seems relevant also. Sociology, psychology, and political science are involved as well as history and philosophy. I think the problem is the extent to which he feels that education has a body of information or sets of ideas sufficiently coherent to warrant very serious study, at least until after students have had extensive experience.

[*] For information about panel members, see Preface, p. x.

DR. HUMMEL: We almost all concurred at lunch that Conant would put the education of teachers into a very condensed period of life, a year of graduate work. He did specify a minimum of undergraduate work in which you learn some sociology, psychology, math, *et cetera*, but this is not especially the education of teachers. You then are apprenticed out to a master teacher for at least 120 clock hours. You work a while just like a carpenter, and presto, you are a teacher. This almost seemed to some of us to make a trade out of the teaching profession. This denies that we have any content or theory of the knowledge of learning. These things are just ignored.

DR. READ: I wouldn't say "ignored." Conant clarified this yesterday when he also said that he considers education a profession. I think there is a need to distinguish his undergraduate program from what he suggests should follow the apprenticeship I believe he would defend the professional aspects of the undergraduate level by saying one first becomes a professional historian, chemist, and so forth. Then, after finishing student teaching, one can get the theoretical foundations when they will be more meaningful in light of practice. Finally, at the end of the probationary period plus the master's degree, one has achieved the professional level. But I do think that his undergraduate program is purely preparation for an apprenticeship.

DR. KIRCHER: Conant seems to hold the conventional belief that the substantive studies should take place only in the basic disciplines of the arts college. Strictly adhered to, this would emasculate much of the profession we like to think we are developing. I believe this position requires extreme faith in a clinical professor upon whom he then places an impossible burden.

DR. BRUBACHER: A recent book concludes that we are not a discipline, but must rely on other disciplines because we haven't got a defined body of knowledge and a distinct way of doing research to expand our knowledge.[1]

DR. WAYLAND: I concur with that point of view, but I don't think it necessarily follows that Conant's approach will then aid us to improve our schools. His program lacks a structure to facilitate research and in the absence of a number of people devoting themselves to this, we will not extend our knowledge. This is the critical matter to me—to improve our task—whether we talk about education as a discipline or not.

DR. TEMPERO: Conant seems to stress subject-teaching, to neglect behavior changes as a prime goal, and to feel that any liberal arts graduate may teach.

DR. BRUBACHER: Aren't we really vulnerable here? We all teach theory, but how many of us do it so as to affect our students' teaching?

DR. PARKER: We are more prone to be alert to social realities, civic responsibilities, and school problems than are academicians. It seems to me that Conant wants academicians to be more involved in teacher education, something they haven't been generally active in for a long time. My point is that if they want more responsibility, they need to prepare for it by becoming more aware of the social and technological needs of society as a whole. Insofar as educational theorists have done this, they have been building toward professional status. Academicians entering the education field will have to replow ground that we are now plowing.

DR. BRUBACHER: The medical clinician takes his students into the wards where they apply their learning. Most education theorists don't do this. We turn it over to supervising teachers who don't know much theory, and we know little practice. Doesn't Conant have us here?

DR. KIRCHER: I think so. The low correlation between successful performance in our classes and in the field is something we don't like to discuss, but as far as we are from dealing effectively with practice, I am convinced that the arts college is still further away. Happily many students in schools of education do undergo a reorientation of their whole attitude. They start looking forward to their profession with a sense of its importance; some start rearranging their ideas and the way they use them not merely as college students, but also as future teachers.

DR. TEMPERO: I think we find this in medical or dental or law school.

DR. BRUBACHER: In law school a fellow can serve a clerkship largely in the office, not out in the courts which are more akin to the wards.

DR. KIRCHER: I think Conant starts one becoming a teacher entirely too late for the orientation we feel necessary.

DR. WAYLAND: There is a fundamental difference between the clinical situations in medicine and education which makes the comparison faulty. The medical clinician works with an individual patient and makes a diagnosis of that particular case; teachers who move into school systems are joining social organizations with ongoing patterns of action in which what they do is already set in the system. I would argue that the induction of teachers is not simply a matter of learning how to teach a particular subject or level, but also of learning the "norms" of an ongoing system. Conant is capitalizing upon this sociological dimension without being explicit about it. Our whole history shows it is possible for people to move into the system and teach, even though they cannot formulate a philosophy and lack knowledge of children and of their community. The practice-teaching emphasis is quite appropriate because the system makes it possible for the person to learn enough in apprenticeship to take the place of someone who was there previously. But I maintain that this is an insufficient goal.

DR. READ: I am bothered by Conant's simple presentation and analysis of what he grants is a very complex situation. His book seems directed not to people who have a depth of understanding of education, but to the public and members of boards of education who do not care to get into the theoretical aspects of the problem. He confirmed this yesterday when he stated that, unlike in Germany, metaphysics isn't held to be significant to education in the United States. I think his proposal is pretty much what you would find in the preparation of German secondary school teachers, omitting only the metaphysical philosophy and history of the German program. Conant deals with means rather than ends, and doesn't really accept the formative idea of a science. Perhaps that is why he has very little good to say of the foundations area. He thinks education should be reduced to a science; that as yet we don't have much in the way of solid knowl-

edge; and that the whole matter of teaching really
doesn't involve much more than a chemist teaching
adolescents chemistry. I think he treats it very superficially.

DR. HUMMEL: I somewhat rejected the suggestion that
many professors lack the practical knowledge and
that many supervisors of student-teaching lack theory. I think we sell ourselves short here, and that Conant has sold us short. For my part, most education
teachers are pretty well grounded in school operations. For some time I have had faith in the practical
and theoretical knowledge of those who supervise
clinical work, and this has been considerably
strengthened here in Chicago. I think that Conant
hasn't realized that we do have clinical professors in a
few places, and that what we need is to increase the
number of supervisors who are well versed in theory.

DR. BRUBACHER: How many historians actually know
whether what they teach is made use of in the public
schools?

DR. HUMMEL: Our institution has them supervising the
high school teachers.

DR. BRUBACHER: How many teachers of educational history, philosophy, psychology, or sociology see whether
their students use the theory?

DR. KIRCHER: How many of those teaching theory can
enliven it with a constant reference to the daily problems of teachers and with a factual and realistic
understanding of the schools and the contemporary
problems they face? I may have met some different
educational philosophers than you have, but I believe
much of their teaching could scarcely be distinguished from pure philosophy.

DR. BRUBACHER: Coming back to this oversimplification,

Conant wrote that, when people ask him to define education, fatigue overcomes him before getting started.[2] He then says that he means by education what goes on in school. Why isn't this accepted? Isn't it empirical and straightforward enough? There is a certain kind of realism about this, isn't there?

DR. KIRCHER: Isn't it a tradition in higher education to smile when a major discipline proposes to define education or when someone within a discipline suggests that there is a certain definition that all should accept? They have a faith in the humanistic tradition in the study of history and literature, the scholarly tradition. They are involved in the process but consider it a boring waste of time literally to define it. And Conant may well be right that no final definition will ever be attained. Perhaps what makes Conant weary is the pretension of some professional educators who sound as if they finally had this definition in the bag.

DR. BRUBACHER: Do you think Conant views psychology as a more dependable source of educational theory than history, philosophy, or sociology?

DR. KIRCHER: I think he is drawn more to psychology but I think he is intuitively drawn to history and philosophy except that he doesn't see why they should be in a department or college of education.

DR. PARKER: My main point would be that history departments have not dealt with the history of education. Some historians have been concerned with the history of philanthropy and how philanthropy affects education. Some have written on the history of economics, but not necessarily on how economics affects education and school plants. The same thing can be said about philosophy departments where the main concern is theoretical. You find very few philosophy departments with a philosopher of medicine or a philosopher of law.

DR. BRUBACHER: There are courses in jurisprudence in law school.

DR. PARKER: Yes, with good reason. My observation is that the academic disciplines have avoided studying the complicated structure of American public education. History departments have not been willing to wrestle with the history of educational problems. These are very complex.

DR. BRUBACHER: A few years ago, a committee from the American Philosophical Association and one from the Philosophy of Education Society agreed that people in educational philosophy should qualify as academic philosophers and that academic philosophers who were to teach educational philosophy should have seriously studied education.[3] Wouldn't this be a good approach?

DR. WAYLAND: I am not sure. Conant made a statement which, if taken literally, marks him as a revolutionary: "As in the case of the employment of clinical professors, it is high time that the faculties of education shook off the self-imposed shackles of academic traditions, borrowed from faculties of arts and sciences."[4] As a group which has always felt inferior, we simply adopted the structure of the arts and sciences faculty with its academic courses and credits. Other forms might be more effective. If we had to make the role of the clinical professor real, I think the consequence in time would be a major restructuring of the whole process of teacher preparation. In this context, then, the question of the way the historian or the sociologist relates to that new structure would be quite different from what it is now. I must admit that I, and I think it true of most of my colleagues here, try to give as good courses as the "pure" ones. We feel that we must do this, even though this may not be the form which makes the greatest technical contribution. It may be good general education; it is a moot question whether it is good education for preparing teachers.

DR. TEMPERO: Conant is a conservative in that he wants academicians to teach the foundations while knowing they have not studied the problems of students.

DR. WAYLAND: I think you are right. He really is engaged in a political process of trying to move the area a stage or two further rather than prescribing what he might consider desirable long-range goals. Even if he does not take his statement seriously, I think we should. Are, for example, foundation courses simply general professional education or do they have instrumental value?

DR. BRUBACHER: You call education a profession rather than a discipline.

DR. WAYLAND: We ought to speak about the job to be done, not the symbols.

DR. READ: Maybe Conant is right. In observing education colleges, I have found that the people who are teaching history and philosophy of education all too often are not very solidly grounded. We have been dominated by the service concept of education. We feel we have to teach these required courses; hence some colleges assign any professor who has a few free hours to fill out the program. I know of a case where a specialist in school law was assigned to teach a philosophy of education course just to fill out his summer schedule.

DR. TEMPERO: I don't think subject mastery alone equips

a person to teach. He also needs an understanding of how children grow and develop.

DR. READ: I am bothered by Conant's suggestion that the graduate school be open to anyone who has a bachelor's degree and is teaching. If I understand him correctly here, I think he hasn't thought through the consequences for the graduate school very carefully. I don't know of a graduate school in the United States that really would lower itself to this entrance criterion unless we assume that we will get every one into teaching who is in the upper third of the class, which Conant suggests. But I think this unrealistic.

I think we ought to allocate advanced work in education to two basic institutions: one geared to service and the other to research. The first would be a post-graduate school or institute where we would admit everyone who is teaching for advanced courses in theory or practice. One could get a Master of Teaching degree and a Doctorate of Education, and these programs would fulfill certification requirements. This institute would be separated and quite distinct from the graduate school which would stress scholarly research and lead to a Ph.D. Presently, with every change in certification requirements, we juggle our education courses in graduate school to get the students ready for a principalship or a guidance position, and this is corrupting the graduate education curriculum and the purpose of a graduate school.

DR. BRUBACHER: Would you suggest our Society police its membership along a more strict definition of subject matter lines? Conant recommends this for high schools and the same might apply then in the university.

DR. READ: I think Conant is correct in this.

DR. TEMPERO: I am not sure but what this is neo-Conant.

DR. READ: I said he treated it superficially.

DR. KIRCHER: Wayland, does your idea of what we could be doing favor a person accomplished in philosophy and in philosophy of education utilizing that equipment for thinking through and helping to solve the critical problems of education today, instead of teaching philosophy as he was taught?

DR. WAYLAND: Having made the kind of statement that I did, one might logically assume that I have a clear picture of what this better system would be. I must say that I do not. We are just beginning to raise some of the questions about the character of our operation which should have been raised a hundred years ago. Until we obtain a larger body of knowledge about what goes on in teaching, learning, and the nature of the school setting, it seems to me we are handicapped in terms of what we can do. We need to know a great deal more about some of the fundamental dimensions of our task before we can make the kind of specific relationship between the larger and more abstract concepts and the particular problems in the field. This is the problem to me, and it involves a certain level of understanding of all of the disciplines represented here. Meanwhile, the education faculty must continue to operate, to push its research ahead, to give direction to the research of social scientists, and to give their energies collectively and individually to building the knowledge upon which to construct and operate newer modes of teacher education.

DR. TEMPERO: Are you saying we have moved further in the disciplines than practitioners have moved in understanding school problems?

DR. WAYLAND: In a sense we technically have the tools
to do that whereas they may not. It seems to me that
the professionally trained psychologist is in a better
position to do this research in education than the curriculum specialist, the teacher of chemistry or reading, or the supervisors who are not likely to have mastered the necessary social–science techniques. We
have a responsibility to take the leadership in developing this body of knowledge and to involve
practitioners in this process.

DR. HUMMEL: Perhaps Mr. Conant has proposed a
method of teacher education not based on a study of
the characteristics of our schools. Is his undergraduate pattern, with its lack of background courses, adequate to send twenty-year olds out to teach not only
academically sound young people but also those of
lesser ability and those from deprived homes?

DR. BRUBACHER: Is there a political motivation behind
Conant's program?

DR. WAYLAND: I would say political in that it is an exercise in the examination of the possible. Here is a man
deeply devoted to American education and the American way of life. Like many university presidents of
the last century but very few academicians in the last
generation, Conant has a deep concern about the
school system. He has said in effect that he wants to
find the best way of moving in the real world, not to
pose a system so different from our present one that
there is no chance of its being taken seriously. He has
made a kind of analysis, trying to locate critical points
in the system which might be modified, hoping these
might lead to even more changes. It has to be judged
a political movement, but it doesn't represent a radical shift from our present approach.

DR. BRUBACHER: You may remember that Conant described himself as a revolutionary, but Harold Taylor said he is a conservative. Wayland, it seems to me that you are saying he is essentially a conservative in that his proposed program is built in the contemporary culture rather than looking ahead.

DR. HUMMEL: I think it is very conservative.

DR. PARKER: Conant is the last of a long list of investigators financed by the Carnegie Foundation for the Advancement of Teaching founded in 1905. This foundation under Henry S. Pritchett designated a number of professions for improvement, and I think Pritchett, followed by Frederick R. Keppel, had in mind medical education, engineering education and other professions including teacher education. After World War II, Conant was selected because of his stature and prestige to investigate the junior high school, the high school and now teacher education. I think that the shock of his last report is wholesome.

DR. KIRCHER: I think Conant is every now and then most refreshing, coming at the whole thing freshly, because he gets the kinds of ideas that wouldn't occur to us. I think his very innocence of much of professional education allows him insights; for example, one that shocked me—that no one in American education had ever designed a successful program for the slow or below-average learner from kindergarten through high school. We may have in theory, but we have not done so in fact. And in the professional schools in which we live, we are not much impelled to concentrate on this.

DR. READ: Is it possible that Conant has caught us in a transition between Jacksonianism and Jeffersonianism? Most of us in foundations were trained in the twenties, thirties, and early forties when egalitarian democracy was the frame of reference in our public school work. The liberal was identified with the common man and a dedication to educating him. Now the liberal is saying, "We are the elite; we will lead the common man." We have inherited a theory which is not in accord with the value orientation now taking over American education.

DR. BRUBACHER: Harold Taylor said that Conant stresses the controversy between the professionals and the academicians, while Taylor claims the important matter to be the role of the school in society.

DR. READ: I would advocate developing theory that has no relationship to practice. We ought to have pure educational theory just as we have a pure science. We ought to develop this as an area where we aren't worrying about practical implications. I think too many of our educators are pragmatically oriented.

DR. BRUBACHER: How about pure pragmatists?

DR. HUMMEL: These too are going to have a discipline and a profession; on this wing of the panel, we are going to have it all one.

DR. WAYLAND: At this point I'd like to predict the response of the profession to the Conant Report. Within the next year I would predict quite a wide range of reactions: Those people who are hurt the most are going to scream the loudest, and those people whose positions are enhanced are going to be enthusiastic. I would expect those who are active in the Association for Student Teaching to be very happy and those who are deeply involved in NCATE to be quite sour. Those of us in foundations who feel we were shorted are likely to take a somewhat dim view. Liberal arts people are going to ignore it. Individual colleges are going to be active about this but they will not be impelled, however, to do anything about the profession.

DR. READ: My field is comparative education. I feel very left out. Conant doesn't even mention my field. Yet he continually makes judgments in comparative terms and refers to his experiences in Germany, which I think matured him for his invasions into education as a study. I think he is not too anxious to advocate comparative education because as yet we haven't a well-defined discipline.

As I study the English approach to educational reform such as in the Crowther Report and in the very important Robbins report that has just come out, I notice that they approach educational problems quite differently. They have a commission composed of people with divergent views so that their reports have depth, and significant exchange occurs in the committee deliberations. I have a feeling that those who worked with Conant have developed a discipleship. They worked with him to the point that I don't think any of them disagrees with much of what he says. Conant is the "wise old man." He comes to us now with many answers to problems that have challenged the best of experts. He lived in Cambridge and evidently never noticed the slums surrounding Cambridge. Then all of a sudden he catches on and is excited about suburbs and slums in education. As to the foundations area, he says he has never really examined the courses. I think he looked over one or two philosophy of education books and made his judgment. Harry Broudy claims, "Dr. Conant took as his text or pretext the 'worst' book in the philosophy of education and the worst courses." [5]

DR. TEMPERO: Isn't the major problem still the limited time he has in his program with one year of graduate work for all the foundations areas?

DR. HUMMEL: I agree that academicians on our campuses are not going to pay much attention to this book, but I am afraid that off campus too much attention will be paid to it. Dr. Conant occupies a very honored place in our society which will lead many school boards and laymen to accept his word as gospel.

DR. KIRCHER: I do not think that there will be a great many off-campus schoolmen, teachers, superintendents, and principals who will sit down and read the whole thing from beginning to end and deliberate on whether the total package makes sense. They are going to find something here and there that agrees with what they think and then they will quote this authority so that it will get into our public school system in all kinds of strange, little piecemeal bits.

DR. PARKER: Might we not say that this is already in effect through the Master of Arts in Teaching programs which are Conant-oriented?

DR. BRUBACHER: Maybe he got it from them.

DR. PARKER: He started it, I think, at Harvard.

DR. READ: I go to the Soviet Union quite often and I find the same academician-educationist infighting growing there. So I shall take with me Conant's book to create more chaos there. This may be at least one good outcome of the publication. We may end up finding that we in pedagogy have a very close relationship with pedagogues in the Soviet Union. We may have to build bridges with them in our opposition to the academicians.

DR. BRUBACHER: In terminating the panel discussion,

might I suggest a new manifesto: "Pedagogues of the World, Unite!"

Notes

1. John Walton and James L. Kuethe, eds., *The Discipline of Education* (Madison: The University of Wisconsin Press, 1963).
2. James B. Conant, *The Child, the Parent, and the State* (Cambridge, Mass.: Harvard University Press, 1959), pp. 1–2.
3. *Philosophy in the Education of Teachers*, joint report of the Committee on Philosophy in Education of the American Philosophical Association and the Committee on Cooperation with the American Philosophical Association of the Philosophy of Education Society reprinted from *Proceedings and Addresses of the American Philosophical Association, 1958–1959*, XXXII (October 1959).
4. James B. Conant, *The Education of American Teachers* (New York: McGraw-Hill, 1963), pp. 199–200.
5. Harry S. Broudy, "Conant on the Education of Teachers," *Educational Forum*, XXVIII (January 1964), 208.

6

Conant's Fight
for Better Teaching

*Merle Borrowman**

When *The Education of American Teachers*, by James B. Conant, hit the market in September, 1963, Fred Hechinger of the New York *Times* called it "Mr. Conant's bombshell"; to Harold Taylor, erstwhile president of Sarah Lawrence, it was "a P.T.A. manual." Few people have accurately and fully set forth the views which Conant intended to expound. Given the bias which every reader brings to a book, no author can expect all men to find within it the same meaning. But given such widely varying interpretations as *The Education of American Teachers* evoked, one must grant that Conant was less clear than he hoped to be.

Conant tried to speak with the voice of moderation which has characterized his earlier reports on American

* For information about Merle Borrowman, see Preface, p. viii.

education; there is, in the book, balance. But this is an angry book, and the balance is a balance of attack both on the education "establishment" and on those who believe that all problems are solved by the liturgy that "a teacher must above all be a liberally educated man."

The professional educators had, and still have, good reason to assume that Conant was friendly to their aspirations and that he believed the scholarly study of education to be important. Perhaps just because they had so long considered him their friend, they read his book avidly. Many felt threatened because they saw their power base exposed and attacked; others who teach courses in education were personally chagrined because he described much of their work as pathetic.

Moreover, just as the educationists were learning to live with *The Education of American Teachers*, Conant again assaulted their citadel. His new book, *Shaping Educational Policy*, in part derived from the earlier volume, repeated the charges that the National Education Association and its state affiliates seek unwarranted power over teacher education and state departments of education, particularly with respect to programs for elementary and secondary schools. It also seems to suggest that the same groups shape higher educational policy in many states. Unless this suggestion is sharply qualified, it constitutes a gratuitous attack on the N.E.A. coalition and its allies in university departments of education.

Some of the evidence behind *Shaping Educational Policy* does warrant the conclusion that in one or two states generally, and in several states where policy concerning the junior college movement is at issue, the N.E.A. affiliates have played an active role. But if one looks at the nation as a whole, I think it gross exaggeration to consider the educationist establishment a major power factor in the making of higher education policy.

The professors of the arts and sciences and their supporters were not sensitive to Conant's attack. I do not know whether this was because Conant pulled his punches, because they were so self-confident that they failed to conceive themselves subject to criticism, because when the chips are down they are not terribly interested in teacher education, or because they were so delighted to see Conant flail the establishment that they considered his criticism of them mere rhetoric which had to be thrown in so the book would not appear too onesided. My guess is that all four factors were at work. Perhaps Conant's failure to make specific recommendations for basic reform of arts and science education made his criticism seem relatively insignificant.

The most searching critics of *The Education of American Teachers* focused their attention on this and on other things which Conant failed to do. In one sense such criticism is irrelevant. He chose, as any author must, to write at length about some issues, merely to allude to others, and to ignore a further set of issues involved in teacher education. Since the complete reform of teacher education is inseparable from the reform of education as a whole, which is in turn dependent on more fundamental shifts in American culture, no one book can pretend to exhaust the issues. Yet to examine the choices Conant made does help one to understand his book. It also helps set the agenda for further reform of teacher education. Let us first consider the issues which Conant's critics claim did not receive the attention they deserve.

One of Martin Mayer's complaints has to do with the kind of preparation prospective teachers receive in the subjects they are expected to teach. His is not the usual complaint, that teachers in training are required to take too few courses in the liberal arts. Mayer charges that college instruction in the subjects to be taught is not of the right kind. He has been intrigued by the new curriculum movements: the new mathematics, the new physical science, the new biological science, and a new social science curriculum which, it is hoped, scholars will produce. These "new" curricula are the products of many people, but it is fair to say that the group center-ing in Professor Zacharias of M.I.T. has been the most vigorous in developing and publicizing the new pro-grams.

The courses developed by this group and by other curriculum reformers have two things in common: they are the products of university scholars who have worked closely with master teachers on the elementary and sec-ondary school level, and they operate in terms of what are called the "strategies of inquiry" and the "structure of the disciplines," concepts popularized by such men as Jerome Bruner of Harvard.

The new curricula have a third thing in common: if they are to be handled effectively, the teachers in train-ing must have a different kind of academic preparation from what they currently receive. To put it bluntly, most mathematics majors, even from the best colleges, cannot teach the "new mathematics" because it has not been taught to them in college; and the same thing can be said of the other new curricula. Believing as he does that the development of these new courses of study is one of the most important educational advances of the last several decades, Mayer is unhappy because Conant did not spell out the need for serious reform of college curricula.

Mayer is correct in much of his thinking. Though the new courses are subject to considerable improvement, the new curriculum movement itself is tremendously significant. It may well transform American education as dramatically as did the progressive movement of an earlier era. If the subjects taught in the elementary and secondary schools are drastically altered, there must be a major reform of college instruction in these fields.

Though Conant does not give this question the attention some believe it warrants, it is not true that he ignores it. On several occasions he argues that the college and university scholars in each field should work out a program consistent with what they consider the best thought in their disciplines and with what they believe should be taught in the lower schools. The steps already followed by the new curriculum workers, and the next step, recommended by such people as Mayer and Zacharias, the reform of the collegiate curriculum in the specialized fields, are precisely the kinds of moves that would be made by university scholars who took the Conant report seriously. Conant also deplores the resistance such moves have encountered on college campuses.

The second major sin of omission laid by critics at Conant's door is his failure to take more seriously the question of what ought to be the major functions of American schools. Unless we know what the schools *should* seek to accomplish, we can scarcely prescribe the preparation of teachers in those schools. In its most radical form this criticism has been voiced by Harold Taylor. As I understand it, his position is that America faces awesome moral and social crises and that our entire system of education must be drastically reformed or else we shall perish. To write about the education of teachers for a school system already bankrupt, and moreover, to write as if one wanted teachers merely to carry on more effectively the activities in which they are now engaged, is a rather trivial task, in Taylor's view.

On this issue there is a basic conflict between Conant and his critics. Conant is, by no stretch of the imagination, a radical reformer. He is no less sensitive than Taylor to some of the "social dynamite" which lies in our midst. Indeed, in *Slums and Suburbs* he stresses the need for education responses to the problems faced by the urban underprivileged classes. But Conant believes that schools can best contribute to their solution by providing more effective instruction in the traditional arts and sciences and in the vocational fields.

Though more confident than Taylor of the values of traditional instruction, I share his belief that the social functions of the schools should not be taken for granted. We do need to examine radical alternatives for our educational system, and if such alternatives are accepted, then far more drastic reforms of teacher education than those proposed by Conant are in order. I hope Harold Taylor someday writes his book on teacher education. It would be quite different from Conant's book, though the book Conant wrote is of greater value to those holding the Taylor position than they apparently realize. The political reforms suggested by Conant are a necessary condition of more radical reforms which men like Taylor would like to see.

For the past two years Harold Taylor has been a favorite speaker for groups seeking an anti-Conant voice. On each occasion that I have heard him, he has dismissed Conant as concerned with mere political tinkering and has then launched a slashing attack on most of the things for which the educational establishment now stands. I can never understand how so staunch a disciple of John Dewey can treat lightly Conant's efforts to bring about a political situation in which Taylor's ideals stand a chance of being realized. I can, however, understand Taylor's establishment audiences: it is pleasant to dream of new horizons when he who describes the dream neglects to tell you that your own rigidities and vested interests delay its approach.

A more restricted version of the Taylor critique has come from people concerned with instruction in the social foundations of education, namely the history, philosophy, and sociology of education. Perhaps the most astute critic in this group is Edgar Friedenberg of Brooklyn College, although Robert Beck of the University of Minnesota has handled the issue cleverly. These people argue that a teacher who does not thoroughly understand the social forces and ideological commitments which operate in American communities, and who has not consciously examined the bearing of these factors on his behavior as a teacher, is at best a craftsman, incapable of rationally choosing means or ends.

Technically, this criticism is invalid. In connection with what Conant calls "the democratic social component" of a teacher's professional education, he asserts his belief that the teacher must understand the social and ideological forces which bear on the schools. Much of this understanding, Conant maintains, can come from general education in the social sciences. But, he points out, the professors of these subjects often lack an understanding of the schools as part of the social system and have insufficient time to examine educational prob-

lems. For these reasons Conant affirms the desirability
of teachers' taking courses in the history and the philosophy of education.

Yet the conviction clearly stated in his repeated
proposition, "a course in the history or the philosophy
of education is highly *desirable*," is weakened when it is
followed by a qualifier such as "*but not essential.*"

Conant's failure to state clearly his premises concerning the kinds of schools for which teachers should
be prepared, and his failure to insist strongly that teachers in training investigate the relationships between
schooling and social situations, need explanation. As
Robert Beck has pointed out, Conant has written a
number of books in which recommendations for education have been derived from his deep sense of the
American tradition or his acute feeling of contemporary
crisis. These include *Education and Liberty, Education
in a Divided World, Thomas Jefferson and the Development of American Public Education,* and *Slums and
Suburbs.* There is every reason to believe that his values,
his sense of history, and his concern with the problems
of society drive him to study education and attempt its
reform. Why then do some of his critics feel let down?

One can only guess at the answer. Perhaps he believed his own commitments had been adequately
stated earlier, or could be easily inferred from his recommendations. For several years he had written as if
certain reforms—for example, the tightening up of the
secondary school curriculum and action aimed at making slum and suburban schools more responsive to the
conditions of their students—were so obviously needed
that further debate was irrelevant. And it does seem
that Conant often takes for granted that the basic
values of a particular culture are beyond debate. He

had, in *The Child, the Parent, and the State,* expressed the view that abstract general discussions of what "education really ought to be" tend to be fruitless.

I suspect, moreover, that Conant perceived a distressingly large gap between what could potentially be and what is. There are professors who can make the analysis of philosophical, sociological, and educational interrelationships exciting and valuable to a potential teacher. Yet if one is to judge by the reports of teachers in training, not many of them encounter such professors. One hesitates to insist that a course be universally required when one knows that in many cases it will be so badly taught as to be useless. And one wisely refrains from supporting any specific course until one is sure that it will be well related to other instruction the student receives.

The right place to decide what courses will be required is on a particular college and university campus. The right people to make that decision are the faculty members—professional and academic—acting in concert in behalf of the whole university. Such a total faculty knows what it can and cannot do well, and only a local faculty can get behind catalogue descriptions of courses to determine what is actually taught in them.

But a collegiate faculty needs feedback from the field for which it is preparing teachers. Such feedback can be provided by involving state education authorities and public school personnel in appraising the teachers produced by the college. Hence responsibility for the apprenticeship or internship of new teachers must be shared with these other agencies, and machinery must be established whereby weaknesses discovered on the testing grounds—the student-teaching situation—can be brought to the faculty's attention.

The place to decide who should be permitted to teach is the public school classroom where a neophyte begins his teaching as a college student. The right people to make this decision are the public school authorities, headed by the state department of education. The crucial question to be asked by these authorities is not What courses has this person had? but Can he teach?

Interestingly enough, some state education departments interpreted Conant as suggesting that the power of certification be taken from their hands. Such a misinterpretation can be explained on two grounds. In the first place Conant did describe certain state departments as extremely weak. They are. And one can easily assume that Conant would not want to leave major responsibility for determining who should teach in the hands of the weak and inept body. In the second place Conant did describe many state departments as under the control of the N.E.A. coalition, whose power over teacher education he sought to curtail. Their reaction, as well as misinterpretation of his report, suggests that they, too, strongly identify themselves with this group. The new book, *Shaping Educational Policy*, makes clearer his conviction that the solution is to strengthen state departments and to sharpen the focus of their efforts, not to replace them by bodies unresponsive to the public interest.

So far as the N.E.A. coalition is concerned, Conant supported moves which it has long encouraged: the reform of student teaching, and the design of career-development plans for the first three or four years of a teacher's employment. But its members have found it hard to forgive his insistence that neither the National Commission on Teacher Education and Professional

Standards nor the National Council for the Accreditation of Teacher Education should be a major power controlling teacher education and certification.

His attack was particularly distressing for several reasons: the council had already been under the fire of James Koerner in his *Miseducation of American Teachers*; it had just been saved by its appeal committee from a damaging conflict with Carleton College, a high-prestige liberal arts college in Minnesota; the University of Wisconsin had recently launched a vigorous assault on the council; and the national commission formed by colleges and universities to police the accreditation business had already demanded significant changes in the council's structure and policy. All this pressure had come on the heels of the important publication *New Horizons for Teacher Education and Professional Standards,* which had urged "the organized teaching profession" to rely on the council as *the* instrument by which the profession could establish control of teacher education and certification. Thus the council had acquired a symbolic significance far beyond its present virtues or evils.

In the majority of states, it is easier to get a teaching certificate if one graduates from an accredited institution; but it is possible to secure certification without this assistance, and even with it a prospective teacher must eventually fulfill the particular requirements of a given state before he is granted a full certificate. The national council does exert some controls over the organization and the teacher-education programs of institutions it accredits; but very few institutions are completely denied accreditation, and relatively minor efforts are usually sufficient to meet the council's objections. The council does not exist to single out distinguished institutions, or to put poor but hardworking colleges out of business. On its fully approved list are institutions of both types; among those given "provisionally accredited" status are first-rate as well as mediocre colleges; and the few colleges completely denied accreditation are either incredibly bad or thoroughly uncompromising in their determination to maintain their own peculiar pattern.

In my judgment Conant actually pulled his punches in criticizing the national council in his book. But when he spoke before the American Association of Colleges for Teacher Education he charged that some accredited institutions are so poor that no one should dream of automatically certifying their graduates. The supporters of the national council know this, but they believe that in time this evil can be eradicated.

The hope of the N.E.A. coalition is to make sure that no one can teach unless he graduates from an accredited institution, and to maintain the Council for Accreditation of Teacher Education as an autonomous national body largely controlled by groups affiliated with the N.E.A. Only thus, they believe, can the "organized teaching profession" have control of its own membership. Conant's objection to this is threefold: he does not believe an autonomous national body is the proper agency to make universal policy for educating teachers; he does not believe the "organized profession" should have exclusive control over who will be certified to teach; and he does believe that certification should be based on the individual's demonstrated capacity to teach.

There is an interesting irony here. If the Conant proposals were adopted, classroom teachers, the cooperating teachers under whom student teaching is done, would in fact have a veto over every candidate for certification. It is hard to believe, however, that the council gives individual teachers any substantial power over who will be permitted to teach. What is really at stake here is the power of the N.E.A. leadership, not of its membership.

On the council issue there is no evidence that a rapprochement between Conant and his opponents is achievable. The currently proposed reforms still leave the council essentially in the same hands. No member of the N.E.A. coalition has even suggested abandoning the effort to tie state certification to accreditation; at least one of the professional groups, the school administrators, is now limiting membership in its organization to those trained in accredited colleges; and Mr. Conant is still adamantly opposed.

On other matters, however, there is increasing evidence that *The Education of American Teachers* is having an impact. The National Commission on Teacher Education is now encouraging the career-development programs Conant urged for new teachers. Its leaders point out that many of them were thinking along these lines well before the Conant book, and they were. Nevertheless, they publicly acknowledge gratitude to Conant for calling attention to this problem and for creating a climate of opinion in which such improvements become possible.

One professional group, the secondary school principals who remained friendly to Conant throughout the months of controversy, is actually establishing a pilot project of this type in several school systems throughout the nation. In this case explicit recognition is made of Conant's leadership. He and several of his former staff members are assisting the group.

A few states, among them Florida, seem to be loosening up on certification practices without explicit reference to the Conant book. California, Illinois, Wisconsin, and New York are already involved in an experimental program designed to test some of the suggestions made in *The Education of American Teachers*. The project is supported by the United States Office of Education and is administered from the Madison campus of the University of Wisconsin. The colleges involved are the Albany unit of the State University of New York, Sacramento State College in California, the University of Wisconsin at Madison, and Northwestern University. In each state the intent is to design a student-teaching situation which will make it possible for state authorities, public school personnel, and college professors to ascertain whether a particular student teacher warrants certification on the basis of his demonstrated teaching ability. One interesting feature is to determine what differences there may be between the judgments of professors and those of public school teachers. Conant and several of his former staff members have also shared in planning this project.

In New York State the Department of Education, under the leadership of Commissioner James Allen, last November announced a new project involving five public and private institutions. Vassar, Cornell, Brooklyn College, Fredonia State College, and Colgate University are all launching experiments based on Conant's recommendations and conducted with his advice.

Finally, Conant has been in consultation with the faculty of Northwestern University, which is in the early stages of developing what promises to be a radical reform of teacher education, going beyond that contemplated by Northwestern in conjunction with the

Wisconsin project mentioned above. Again, this university is working closely with representatives of the Illinois State Department of Education.

The head of what David Riesman called the "snake-like procession" of higher education begins to turn in the directions indicated by *The Education of American Teachers*. But teacher education is a ponderous and cautious beast. Even when the head moves decisively the body often remains placid. Thanks to Conant and others, that body now lies uncomfortably exposed. Given continued public pressure, it may yet shed its aged and brittle skin to move freely to a more defensible position.

7

Is *The Education of American Teachers* Influencing the Education of American Teachers?

Phi Delta Kappan

PART I—REPORTS FROM KAPPAN * LISTENING POST MONITORS

Twenty-one competent KAPPAN reporters, in all sections of the country, spent several months sampling responsible educational opinion in their own localities to determine how the proposals offered by Mr. Conant were being received and what evidence existed that the book was having any influence.

Our query, "What influence has Mr. Conant's book had in your area?" brought assorted responses. From

* For information about the journal *Phi Delta Kappan*, see Preface, p. vi.

Detroit, "Practically none. There has been no time yet for its influence to be expressed. The TEPS *Position Paper* has had more influence, since it emanated from within the power structure. An outsider must expect to be ignored." From Washington, "There seems to be no question but that Conant's views are being felt, but it may take some time before the implications take root."

A report from Texas asserted that nineteen of twenty-two educators consulted claimed there had been no recognizable influence. Four said the book had caused their faculties to re-examine their programs. Two said it had reinforced decisions already reached. A Minnesota correspondent reported, "There are no drastic plans to alter patterns of teacher preparation here at the university or in any of the neighboring colleges that my colleagues and I are familiar with. There will undoubtedly be minor changes in curriculum as we go along, but I do not see any great new shift in emphasis as a result of Conant's book. It is not having and will not have any appreciable effect on teacher education in these parts." This sentiment is echoed by the Texan who commented, "So far nothing of significance is being planned in this geographic area to alter the pattern of existing teacher preparation programs. True, the policy of tightening up education courses and getting more substance into them is proceeding, but this development had begun long before Conant's book saw the light of day."

The word from Wyoming is that certification will not change appreciably as a result of Dr. Conant's proposals. "TEPS and the College of Education continue to be potent forces, and this will not change."

One reporter quotes an Iowa correspondent who is aware of no changes other than the continuing upgrading that has been going on since 1952, especially requiring bachelor's degrees for elementary teachers and heavier major subject requirements for secondary teachers.

Many areas report a substantial immediate reaction to the book in the appointment of committees and commissions to study it and report to the university faculty, the faculty education council, the governor, the state board of education, or the legislature. Most areas reflect strong personal reactions, with conspicuous mixtures of agreement and disagreement.

Oregon, Washington, and Georgia are reported to have special committee reports being prepared for the state boards of education.

At the University of Nevada as early as last November the University Council resolved that a five-man committee investigate the teacher education program in the light of Conant's suggestions. The committee included the acting dean of education and one representative each from foreign languages, English, history, and physics.

The word from Virginia is that little is being done to alter the pattern of education and Conant's book has had little effect on the little that is being done. However, not many dismissed the book as casually as one Virginia reporter who said, "Mr. Conant's remarks fell under their own weight in our area. Most people dismissed the book from serious consideration." Another Virginian concluded that "Mr. Conant is respected, but not taken too seriously. He seems to be the John Gunther of the education scene, traveling into unknown countries for brief visits, then writing analyses of the forces operating in these areas."

The possibility of influence still to be felt is suggested by another Virginia comment, "The time inter-

val since publication of the book is too short for many
changes to have occurred. The State Board of Education in Virginia has had numerous committees involved
in state-wide studies to improve the quality of teacher
education. Conant's recommendations may influence
the thinking of committee members as they pursue
their work. We prefer this procedure of state-wide committees to Conant's proposal "that each college and university should be permitted to develop in detail whatever program of teacher education it considers desirable."

From Colorado comes a more positive reaction:
"This book is a wonderful example of calm, constructive, incisive criticism. The book needs to be studied
carefully by all sincere students of teacher education to
catch its spirit and ideals without becoming lost in controversy over details and trifles." Colorado reports that
the book has had a discernible influence. Seminars are
using the book as a text. The state department, the general assembly, the state TEPS, the PTA, all are discussing it and measuring their programs against it. Some say
they are already as far in conformity with Conant's
ideas as they can go as an institution. One Colorado
reporter asserts that the book has clearly had these
effects: It has helped to support the hands of admission
officers and others seeking to strengthen teacher education. It has made the public more aware of teacher education problems and has stimulated self-study in the institutions. It is reminding people of the importance of a
commitment by the entire institution. The fact that a
man of Conant's eminence makes such a study raises
the prestige of teacher education.

Less enthusiastic is this Ohio statement, "I think
most of Conant's book could have been written without

any study on his part. The best that can be said is that it is a valuable addition to the literature and will help to focus attention on teacher education. We here in Ohio will not feel any impact for some time, because we already have plenty of unfinished business."

Traces of animosity and hypersensitivity appeared in discussions of the Conant proposals in such remarks as "the presumption of Dr. Conant attempting to be the Supreme Court in American education," "the taking over of free public education by the academicians is as absurd as if I told a surgeon how to operate," and "when you have disposed of the 'temperate' notions of Dr. Conant you ought to evaluate the quackery of men like James Koerner."

A California remark was even stronger, "I think it is an insult to and a tragic commentary on American education that this man, operating as he does, commands such an authoritarian position."

REPORTS REVEAL NO CONFORMITY

One conclusion emerges clearly from the reactions of educators around the nation. The establishment is not devoted to the politics of consensus. Educators are taking their opinions from no one, neither from Conant nor from NEA nor from AACTE nor from NCATE. They are wholesomely deciding for themselves how much Conant they will have, and some are ready to have a great deal and some very much less. Nearly all are heartily in favor of adopting some of the proposals, only there is no agreement on which ones.

One point frequently made by our correspondents was that the constructive suggestions among the many proposals have long been considered and many have been adopted. "That teacher education should be an all-institution function is accepted without any question by the institutions of the State System of Higher Education," says an Oregon correspondent. He goes on to specify, "At Oregon State University the University Council on Curriculum and Academic Policy is the teacher education committee. All curricular proposals affecting teacher education must be submitted for consideration to the council. When the requirements for a teaching major are under consideration, the appropriate academic division appears before the council with its recommendations on the matter. At the University of Oregon, the Teacher Education Committee is an all-institution committee appointed by the president. It consists of sixteen members, nine of whom are from the College of Liberal Arts, three from the school of Education, and four from other professional schools in the university."

The voluminous replies from our Listening Post monitors failed to reveal clear regional differences in the way educators have responded to *The Education of American Teachers*. All sections of the country responded with a mixture of admiration and complaint, and there appears to be no pattern of relation between sections of the country and sections of the Conant plan that meet with approval. From the many assessments of specific Conant proposals, a few samples will indicate the range of the reactions.

A professor of education in Texas says, "The autonomy of the institution in program development under the approved program concept has been clearly demonstrated and proven as a sound theoretical and operational principle. However, to clothe the institution with near-absolute autonomy as a certifying agency is to invite total disunity and disaster. Each institution and its administrative agency would become subject to the manifold pressures of a political and vested interest nature that the author identifies as the causative factors in rendering the state educational agency impotent. Such autonomy would, in effect, be tantamount to a reversion to the era when separate city and county school systems were empowered to issue teaching certificates to any person desiring to teach. Such an arrangement would result in total destruction of every vestige of claim to the professionalization of teaching."

On the same point an education dean in the state of Washington writes, "It is my contention that what exists in the state of Washington meets most of the requirements of Conant's recommendations and does a superior job in comparison. First, the state department has to approve each program of teacher education. There may be 'legitimate' institutions that are of low quality that cannot get approval. This is a safeguard. The state requirements in Washington do not list required courses but, rather, areas; the courses are the prerogative of the institution. The institutions in this state must recommend the candidate for certification before he is certified. This means the institution must be responsible for its product."

Reciprocity in certification among all states brought forth strong rejoinders, of which this one from Oregon is a fair sample: "Dr. Conant's recommendations that the regional and national accrediting associations be deprived of their accrediting powers insofar as these relate to teacher education makes difficult the acceptance of his recommendation that there be reciprocity of certification among the fifty states. The State Department of

Education reports that Oregon annually employs approximately 50 per cent of its teachers from other states. Such teacher mobility suggests the stake Oregon has in the nature of teacher education offered in other states. At this juncture in the development of teacher education, it is our feeling that regional and national accreditation gives us greater assurance of the quality of teacher education programs in other states than we would have without such accrediting agencies. Reciprocity is greatly to be desired, but under appropriate safeguards, such as those afforded by NCATE and regional accrediting associations."

The proposal to eliminate late afternoon and evening courses as a means of qualifying for salary increments elicited strong support and equally vehement opposition. This Florida comment suggests some of the implications: "When Conant proposes that 'Any salary increments based on advanced studies should not be tied to course credits earned (semester hours), but only to the earning of a master's degree and . . . no credit toward the degree should be given for extension courses or courses taken on campus while the teacher is engaged on a full-time teaching job,' he is flying in the face of the current practice. Like many other states, we are enlarging our extension service, establishing new centers, and encouraging teachers to study while they teach. We fail to see the point of Mr. Conant's argument on this point."

Equally controversial is the clinical professor idea. Some comments: "Washington State University has used 'clinical professors' for supervision of student teachers for thirty years. We have several practice teaching centers in the state. The clinical professor lives in the center and supervises and conducts seminars with these students. The period of practice teaching is eight or nine weeks, full time." The University of Wisconsin will adopt the clinical professor plan in the fall of 1964, but had planned it before Conant. The University of Florida is considering the same, but will use the term "clinical specialists."

California schoolmen are understandably less responsive than their colleagues in other parts of the country. Aware that their advice was pointedly ignored in recent state legislation, as well as in the 1962 election, and busily adjusting to recent unwelcome changes in certification standards, California educators did not respond with their accustomed verve.

One of the few conclusions that can be safely drawn from the comments submitted by our twenty-one monitors is that much of the hostility to the proposals offered by Dr. Conant is conservative hostility to any change, since any change is upsetting. A hint of this appears in the statement that "New York observers are confident that the State Board of Education is not about to yield any of its certification authority to the colleges or to anyone else."

Special evidence of the esteem in which Dr. Conant is held lies in the fact that a large number of deans, professors of education, and others, with a fine balance of pride and indignation, make this assertion: "Our college [or our state] probably comes closer than any other to following Mr. Conant's recommendations."

PART II—EDUCATION DEANS REPORT IMPORTANT CHANGES—SOME AS RESULT OF CONANT INFLUENCE

To help identify and assess the impact of *The Education of American Teachers*, KAPPAN editors queried the education deans of AACTE member institutions. The first 320 responses (50 per cent of the mailing) were used for this summary.

One question asked was, "What influence, if any, has James Conant's book, *The Education of American Teachers*, had on your plans?" Forty per cent of the deans (128) admit that there has been some, even if only incidental, influence. This is reflected in such comments as "Little except faculty discussion," "Little except to confirm our own beliefs," and "Dr. Conant's book has encouraged a critical evaluation of our program."

In addition to the 128 deans who admit to some influence on their plans or thinking, ten acknowledge a substantial influence, expressed in remarks like, "We are contemplating a state-wide tryout of the Conant recommendations" (Univ. of Maine), "We now are negotiating a research grant to test Conant's proposals with respect to basing certification on judgments of teaching competence" (Univ. of Wisconsin), and "Dr. Conant's book has had considerable influence in the training of teachers at our institution; however, it has been more in the nature of strengthening a trend which was already in existence than a reversal of present policies" (Gonzaga Univ.).

The ten campuses admitting a substantial Conant

influence included three public and seven private institutions.

Obviously, it is not always possible to identify or recognize the sources of influence, and probably most people have a narcissistic tendency to reject the suggestion that important ideas originated from the outside. To the question, "Have the major forces for change at your institution come from (a) Within your department or school of education? (b) Within your campus, but outside the education department? (c) From educators outside of your own campus? (d) From laymen, outside the profession?," the responses were (a) 280, (b) 105, (c) 86, and (d) 16. Several volunteered the information that NCATE had been helpfully influential.

Although a minority admitted that Dr. Conant's book had affected them, and only a handful were aware of substantial influence, nearly all stated that their teacher education programs were not stagnant. To the question, "What significant changes have been initiated in your teacher education program since 1960?," only one reported no change. Relatively few reported changes that represent mere juggling of schedules or bookkeeping changes. Most of the changes will be applauded for their obvious intent to raise standards and improve quality.

Significantly, a large number of recent changes in teacher education programs accord completely with Conant's recommendations, giving rise to the frequently voiced comment that the most worthwhile of his suggestions are already being practiced and are gaining in institutional favor.

For example, fifty-two colleges reported increased time for student teaching, while only four recorded decreases. Twenty-one reported increased requirements in general education and twenty-nine in subject majors, with none admitting decreases. Sixty-eight claimed to have initiated more selective policies of admission and retention of students in the teacher education program and twenty-two noted the establishment of campus–wide teacher education councils (ten in state institutions, twelve in private).

In addition to the fifty-two announcing greater attention to student teaching, many volunteered information about improvements in this area other than simply devoting more time to it. Fourteen mentioned improved supervision of student teaching; eight claimed to offer better preparatory experience leading up to student teaching; five provide more diversified laboratory experiences; five have integrated methods instruction with student teaching; five have achieved improved cooperation with the school districts; many have moved from an hour-a-day to a half-day or full-day block and from the artificial laboratory school situation into regular schools, and in some cities to substandard districts.

Nearly all of these trends are explicitly or implicitly recommended in *The Education of American Teachers*.

Other innovations noted by the education deans establish clearly that the charge of devotion to the politics of consensus is manifestly untrue if applied to programs and practices in schools and departments of education.

Among the innovations mentioned by one or more institutions were:

Post-baccalaureate paid field experience
Two-year internship for secondary teachers
All seniors will take the National Teachers Examination
The new math required of all elementary teachers

Emphasis on the culturally-deprived child
Introduced an honors system
Revamping of education courses to eliminate overlap
Major in education is being eliminated
New administrative degree of S.I.E. (Specialist in Education)
Established position of Associate in Education
Established resident supervising teacher
The last two devices are strongly suggestive of Dr. Conant's clinical professor idea

About a dozen deans mentioned giving attention to team teaching or television teaching. Eight said they had recently concentrated all professional courses in a single professional semester. Some new programs were reported, chiefly to prepare specialists in the guidance field or for teaching of handicapped children.

Eighteen colleges reported having established an academic subject major requirement for elementary teacher candidates. A large number reported moving to a requirement of two major fields for secondary teachers, reflecting primarily recent legislation in Texas and California. This move is directly counter to Dr. Conant's suggestion that high-school teachers should be prepared and assigned in one field only.

Since questionnaires to education deans asked broad and open-ended questions, and since the space allotted for answering was severely limited, we know that the answers are not at all accurate in respect to the number of institutions participating in the various changes mentioned. This was not designed as a statistical study, but merely as a sampling of ideas current in teacher education.

Some of these ideas are better revealed by direct

quotations from the deans than by attempts to compile and generalize. Some samples:

"We have also received a supplemental grant from the Ford Foundation to continue our experimentation with a certification by examination plan which we had had in operation for three years. We have also requested support for a project designed to focus on the student teaching experience in line with Conant's recommendations. We are going to implement his recommendations on the clinical professor beginning in September of 1964, although this is something which we have been thinking about. We believe that while most of our direction had been arrived at prior to the publication of Mr. Conant's book, the wide dissemination of his recommendations has stimulated our faculty to further action and lent support to our program developments" (Wisconsin).

"Introduction of two-year internship program for secondary school teachers. Summer program of practice teaching and curriculum and methods, followed by a full year of teaching at a carefully selected secondary school. Cooperating teachers in this internship are paid by the university and selected jointly by school and university. Second year of study is full year of graduate work at university with student enrolled in both the faculties of education and the arts and sciences. Completion of the program leads to the Master of Arts in Teaching degree. We have kept our one-year programs leading to the same degree" (Harvard).

"Developed an experimental program in professional education, eliminating all professional courses as such and using the psychological approach with a team of instructors dealing with problems and issues in higher education. Inaugurated a three-year study of concepts to be developed in teacher education, which will lead to revision of the education sequence" (Florida).

"In the junior year courses once identified as psychology, methods, and tests and measurements are taught as an integrated whole by a team of teachers representing these disciplines. In the area of principles, educational philosophy, and adolescent or child psychology, the same approach is made. Teachers are college staff members from each area concerned and the classroom supervising teacher who is involved with the student teacher" (Tuskegee Institute).

"Each of several blocks of work is taught by a team of professors (three or four) who are specialists in the phase which they teach. These professors plan the work so that the students get the phases of work appropriate to their needs, but duplication and overlapping is kept at a minimum. The secondary methods block is offered during the first seven weeks of the semester in which the student teaching is done. The same professors who teach the methods block supervise student teachers in their own subject field during the last nine weeks of the semester." (American Univ.).

PART III—STATE SUPERINTENDENTS DISSENT

The responses of state superintendents' offices reflect continuing action to strengthen certification standards for teachers, and very little enthusiasm for the Conant proposals.

Of forty-five states reporting to Phi Delta Kappa,

only four (Hawaii, Mont., Nev., Wyo.) stated that there had been no significant changes in certification standards in their states since 1960.

Of these forty-five respondents only three (Utah, Alaska, N. Mex.) clearly approve Conant's plan for basing certification on a recognized bachelor's degree, success in a state-approved student teaching program, and recommendation by the preparing institution. Only nine (Colo., Maine, Neb., N. Mex., Penn., R. I., W. Va., Fla., Calif.) unreservedly support the suggestion of certification reciprocity among the states. Many others expressed qualified support, but with qualifications so substantial that they amount to a different proposal.

The beefing up of standards has been mostly in directions congenial to the Conant thinking. While one state, Alaska, reported raising the requirements in professional courses, and one state, Indiana, increased the requirements in student teaching, at least nine now demand more units in the teaching field than they did in 1960 (Conn., Fla., Calif., Idaho, Okla., Vt., Va., Wis., W. Va.) and at least six have raised the general education standards (Calif., Ind., N. Y., Ohio, Okla., Penn.).

Other recent changes in certification rules include the establishment of new credentials for social workers in Indiana, for librarians in Massachusetts, for guidance workers in Georgia and Kansas, and for special education in Georgia and Indiana. Texas has passed more stringent regulations regarding the assignment of teachers to areas in which they are fully prepared, and South Carolina has added a requirement in either state history or modern mathematics.

One state, Maryland, has made provision for certification on the basis of graduation from and recommendation by an NCATE-approved institution.

Four states have for the first time required that all teachers be graduates of four-year colleges (Ala., Ark., Mo., Ky.), and six states have adopted five-year programs for the full credentialing of teachers, though the fifth year need not be completed before beginning teaching.

It should be pointed out that additional upgrading of certification standards has taken place in other states, and that the figures cited here represent incomplete reporting. Responses were received from forty-five states, but eight of these were in the form of bulletins too lengthy to be analyzed in time for this report.

Typical of American educational thinking today is the diversity of aims in the various states. An open-ended question asking, "What changes would you like to see adopted in your state or throughout the nation?" brought twenty-seven responses which included sixteen distinct suggestions. Among the changes desired by several state department offices were: extension of reciprocity of comparable programs, 5; accreditation of approved programs, 4; universal requirement of a bachelor's degree, 4; and fewer certificates, with less specificity, 2.

Relatively few states have specific changes planned for the foreseeable future, though two states admit aiming at the bachelor's degree minimum, two are working towards a five-year program, and several are planning minor revisions. Far more significant is the fact that at least a half-dozen states, which means probably a dozen in all, have general revisions in mind. They have complete restudies underway, but do not know what recommendations will ensue. These states are likely to be influenced by the Conant proposals, and a number have held conferences and symposia devoted specifically to reports and analyses of the Conant plan, most of which were unfavorable.

Typical of evidence that the book is having substantial influence, regardless of how many of its proposals are ultimately adopted, is this excerpt from a letter from a state superintendent:

"While we are aware that the Colorado General Assembly has discussed the book, we have been advised that this body will authorize a restudy of the Teacher Certification Act of 1961 during the 1964 calendar year. It is inevitable that the study will take into account at least some of Conant's recommendations. The legislative council during 1963 mentioned the book several times, and it may be that the book served as a spark to convince the General Assembly that it was time to take a second look at our certification law.

"Judging from the testimony of Colorado teachers in two days of open hearings before the Colorado Committee on Educational Endeavor on November 6–7, 1963, I would conclude that the book has been widely read in Colorado collegiate institutions and that the reading has not been limited to the faculty in education. At the moment I am not aware of any significant changes on any of the campuses, but such changes are notoriously slow in evolving, so that another assessment of the impact of the book on Colorado collegiate campuses should be made a year or two hence."

The director of certification for Nebraska offers an evaluation typical of several: "Dr. Conant has made a significant contribution to teacher education. Many of his recommendations will no doubt [be adopted]. Others were in the planning and early implementation stages when the report was released." In a similar vein is the comment from Massachusetts: "I believe the study, the report, and the ensuing controversy have been good for the profession, and will result in improved teacher preparation. Dr. Conant's reputation will serve to focus the attention of the public and the profession on the inadequacies of some programs and will give impetus to efforts being made to correct them."

Such positive reactions far outnumbered those from state department officials who feel threatened, as apparently the author of this one does: "The Conant report if adopted will make teaching a craft rather than a profession. It will place control of teacher education in the hands of subject matter professors and academicians. The general effect will be to greatly weaken, if not destroy, professional education."

Far more typical are the comments from the Connecticut official who wrote, "Most of us find it hard to disagree with Conant's (or Koerner's, for that matter) *findings*. His recommendations, however, are conceived for a Panglossian 'best of all possible worlds,' which we are far from achieving, even in the enlightened state of Connecticut. Given such a world, most of the recommendations, if put into effect at one time, might result in considerable improvement over the present state of affairs; but then, so, *per se*, would the existence of a better world.

"Teacher certification is indeed much too cumbersome, and the time is rapidly approaching in some states when the protective function, heretofore the exclusive burden of the state through certification, is going to have to be shared very heavily by the 'profession' at large, if the quotes are ever to be removed. The crutch that has been certification is weakening, and the cripple is going to have to walk with no more than a cane."

8

The Issues, the Impact, the Philosophies

Robert M. Weiss

I AN HISTORICAL PERSPECTIVE

Rapid social change and differences about educational policy have characterized American society. Educational questions in colonial America centered on whether to alter the transplanted European patterns. At the end of the seventeenth century, Governor William Berkeley thanked God that Virginia had neither free schools nor printing presses to lead to heresy and disobedience of established authority. A hundred years later Jefferson's "Bill for the More General Diffusion of Knowledge" was defeated by the Virginia legislature. But that was a short-lived conservative triumph. Educational expansion has generally accompanied the development of American society. Each year, a larger proportion of the population is schooled for a longer period within the year and for a greater number of years. Education has become an increasingly larger personal and public financial investment. Simultaneously, there has been greater public concern with the nature of education. No time in American history has witnessed both more schooling and more debate about it than the years since the Second World War.

The war contributed both directly and indirectly to the accelerated postwar focus on education. The war had revealed through Selective Service tests the educational defects of a large percentage of the population. Rebuilding the society became linked to rebuilding the schools. "Return to normalcy" meant a return to concern for domestic affairs. The war had diverted materials to the battlefield. It discontinued the schooling and disrupted the lives of multitudes. The G.I. Bill was one attempt on the part of the federal government to close the education gap created by the war.

A shortage of school personnel and outmoded facilities resulted from the plowing of the nation's human and economic resources into the all-out war. Just as the Civil War had stimulated the industrial age of iron and steel, so the Second World War accelerated the technological atomic age. More intellectual and more specialized skills are required in the automated age than our educational system was geared to produce. Today there is a great awareness of this shortage and of the increased dependence on schooling to meet this need. A high postwar birth rate enlarged school enrollments. Metropolitan populations continue their enormous expansion, especially of school-age youth in both suburbs and slums.

There is a subtle and thus very pervasive way by

which wars, especially hot and unlimited ones, injure people by perverting their sense of values. The late Donald G. Tewksbury began his class on "Education and World Community" at Teachers College, Columbia University by writing on the board: "In times of war, truth is the first casualty." As dollars and personnel were deployed to fight the military conflicts, so ideas became weapons in the ideological struggles. The relatively new field of psychology contributed to the war with improved testing methods and massively-used propaganda techniques. In such an atmosphere, the question of the validity of a concept became subservient to the matter of which side it would serve. Unless seen as directly contributing to the war, new and different ideas were both repressed and suppressed. Reality became markedly skewed so as to bolster the patriotic spirit of angelic purity versus the devil enemy. This "black and white" approach carried over to the Conant controversy. Debates about Viet Nam policy in the 1960s also seem to illustrate that national defense and intellectual defensiveness tend to go together.

"The Age of Suspicion" (as James Wechsler, former editor of the *New York Post*, entitled his book about the McCarthy period), has markedly declined, but elements of it persist, as Arthur Schlesinger, Jr. pointed out in *The Saturday Evening Post* (August 13, 1966). The surrender of Germany and Japan did not entirely dissipate the hostile attitudes and military-mindedness that had been so greatly reinforced by the improved mass media. The current popularity of espionage and Western movies and television programs indicates they are serving a sociological as well as a psychological function. The realignment of nations into Cold War participants may be more a consequence of the large scale hot one than is currently realized. The McCarthy era might better be conceived of as a predictable postwar social phenomenon than as merely the influence of a megalomaniac, just as Hitler's rise to power should be interpreted in light of the social and cultural factors which made Nazism appealing.

The postwar social milieu led initially to what Ernest O. Melby dubbed "American Education Under Fire" in his 1951 pamphlet, and William W. Brickman called "Attack and Counterattack in American Education" in an article that same year.[1] Loyalty oaths increased after the Second World War and much of postwar American educational history has been marred by academic freedom problems. As Willis Rudy termed it (see note 43 in Chapter 1), "The 'Cold War' Among American Educators" results from the transformation in the larger cultural context. But with cold wars and limited wars replacing hot and unlimited ones, there has also been the reassertion of conflicting views. Challenged were the optimistic Jacksonianism of progressive educators and the Deweyan philosophy of pragmatism with its many interpretations and misinterpretations. The idea of the worth of the individual as an end in his own right has become transformed into a concern with the individual's contributions to "hot" or "cold" wars and to a corporate technological society.

Once again, as Lawrence A. Cremin documented in *The Transformation of the School*, the criticisms of progressive school theories and practices reflected the decline of the climate of social reform which persisted between the Depression and the start of the Second World War. The postwar period brought with it a reaction against the demands for radical social change that had been so dominant in the thirties and forties. In the fifties, progressive educators were blamed not only for all the shortcomings in the teaching of fundamental skills but also for the increased delinquency, and the substitution of soft and relative standards for firm discipline and absolutes. They had attempted to replace the supposedly "tried and true" first principles with an experimental approach. They had sought basic socioeconomic changes and as Robert E. Mason depicted in *Educational Ideals in American Society* (1960), they were confronted in the postwar period by the opposition of the new conservatives. Even the patriotism of the progressives was questioned in such reactionary pamphlets as *How Red is the Little Red School House?* [2]

There was an increase of those who viewed the progressive stress on "functional" curriculum revision and the developmental approach as detracting from essential content generally defined as the traditional academic subjects. In 1956, the Council on Basic Education was organized to stress the fundamental disciplines in contrast to the progressive child or society-centered or combined "life-adjustment" approaches. To many, not merely Conant, a reassertion of concern with subject matter and academics appeared overdue. As physicist Jerrold Zacharius' and psychologist Jerome Bruner's recent contributions on theories of learning and instruction illustrate, the new curriculum revision focuses on the organizing and structuring of content in a field so as to provide an intellectual experience for learners at a particular stage of development. Frequently in the history of education, aspects neglected in one age are stressed at a subsequent time.

The technological demands and the accompanying growing enrollment in higher education have helped strengthen the reemphasis on subject matter as related to the basic concepts in the particular field under consideration. These societal trends have also increased the value of each stage of schooling primarily as it contributes to a later one. The "new math" is acknowledged by many in the field to be mainly a reorganization concentrating on older Platonic mental disciplinary goals in contrast to the "progressive" emphasis on immediate function and use. The federal government has instituted what is called "Operation Headstart." I prefer the term "Operation Enrichment" because by stressing *present* enrichment over preparation for *future* school and life competition, the latter may actually be better accomplished. Either way, these preschool experiences are designed to assist the "culturally deprived" children of the poor to compete effectively in school and thus to enhance their chances for success in later life. Such opportunities are necessary because the public schools have not established such programs for all children. While most nursery school personnel emphasize acceptance of the child more than intellectual achievement, one extreme exception is Isabelle P. Buckley who wrote a book entitled *College Begins at Two* (1965). Opposition persists between the two emphases although there is a need for a balanced blend of concern with the child as child and in relationship to his adult future. According to psychiatrist Eric Berne, author of *Games People Play* (1964), all people are made up of an internalized parent, adult, and child aspect, and it is the natural child aspect (as opposed to the child adapting to or against his parents) which is the source of adult creativity. His theories urge us to give up childish conformity or rebellion, but to retain the awe, wonder, creativity, and vibrancy of our childlike aspect.

The schools have failed to reduce significantly the

opportunity differential between the children of the poor and those from families of higher socioeconomic background. Schools have not only started too late, but the nature of their methodology and programs favor upper-status youth. As Evans Clinchy, director of the Office of Program Development of the Boston Public Schools, has said:

The money poured into Title I (of the Elementary and Secondary Education Act) is largely going to be wasted if we continue to spend it on bolstering the present system of educating children. . . . Title I has to become much more directed toward breaking the established habits and patterns that have proved themselves totally incapable of even helping, much less educating, disadvantaged children. If this requires Congress to rewrite the title, so be it. But simply to assist the present system to do in a more elegant way what it is already doing so badly is to pervert the possibility of what American education should and could be.[3]

In one of his cartoon strips, Jules Feiffer satirized the trend emerging from the increased importance of schooling in determining occupational roles and social position. The strip began with two parents discussing what college their son should attend; it ended with their noting that soon he would be starting kindergarten. There are now greeting cards for graduation from kindergarten and even for just getting promoted from any grade. Concern with preparing students for later levels of schooling through earlier ones is necessary and has merit but not when it totally replaces consideration of what pupils are inherently gaining at each stage. As Wilford M. Aikin's *The Story of the Eight-Year Study* of the Progressive Education Association (1942) showed with high school students in relationship to college, those educational experiences immediately significant to the learners may be the ones which best prepare for later schooling.

Conant stresses the "ladder" concept of schooling. He is concerned with stages of childhood mainly as these relate to later adulthood and with levels of schooling as these contribute to higher ones. This is in contrast to the child-centered progressives who emphasized the present stage of development of the learner, and to existentialists who also stress the present. The existentialists focus on the immediate responsible choicemaking of the individual defining his self and his humanness. They do not especially distinguish between childhood and adulthood and have begun only recently to speak directly, but reticently, to the matter of child rearing. In the manner of Rousseau, they have tended to see a concern with child rearing as meaning authoritarian adult imposition on children's human development. To this writer, an adequate education requires attention to past traditions, present stages, and future consequences.

At the 1963 Philosophy of Education Society annual meeting, Professor M. I. Berger of the State University of New York at Albany seems to have been the first to note the absence of any existential thought in Conant. Berger, in comparing *Slums and Suburbs* to the writing of James Baldwin, says: "It is the difference between the objective report of an inspector-general and the impassioned confession of an individual. It is the difference between *Dasein* which for Jaspers and Heidegger represents what is commonplace in human existence and *Existenz*, that which is breathtaking." [4] In his admittedly exaggerated attack, Berger pointed out that Conant stressed surveys, percentages, the status quo, trends; was overly serious, lacking in passion, originality, and courage; and that he thinks of the Negro as a social force (rather than as an individual human) whom he wants to uplift as part of his "Yankee liberalism."

By the time Conant did his teacher education study, the attacks and criticisms of public education had changed focus from the schools to questions about the education of teachers. In 1963, only a few months before *The Education* was published, James D. Koerner released his *The Miseducation of American Teachers*. Koerner had been executive director and was at that time president of the board of directors of the Council for Basic Education. Although based on a two-year exploration of both the literature and conditions (sponsored by the Relm Foundation of Ann Arbor, Michigan), his book was more polemical and vitriolic and less scholarly and cautious than the Conant work. In *The Miseducation*, Koerner used a study written by this writer (on grading in education courses); Koerner included only data that supported his case, and omitted data and explanations that countered his point.[5] Koerner did little but engender the hostility of professional educators. He was grouped by educationists with Arthur E. Bestor, Jr., John Keats, Albert Lynd, Admiral Hyman Rickover, Max Rafferty and Mortimer Smith as generally hostile and unwelcome critics. They were depicted as staunch educational conservatives either transferring their prestige in other areas of competency to professional education or in the case of Rafferty, as simply expressing a dangerously extreme right-wing outlook. They were not dismissed as disreputable attackers as had been the case with Alan A. Zoll, former aide to Father Coughlin and others.[6]

Conant's stature was too great for his critics to succeed in dismissing his viewpoint on such grounds, although a few tried. Coming as it did in September at the beginning of the school year, *The Education* exemplified Conant's excellent political timing and almost totally eclipsed Koerner's book. In the 1950's Conant had continued to assert himself as a loyal public-school supporter. In one review, he had lashed out at the crisis in Pasadena, California that had resulted in the firing of Superintendent Willard Goslin; a year later, Conant suggested that critics of public schools should be evaluated as friends or foes in terms of whether they wanted to increase the financial support of public education or to drain money from it for private schooling.[7] No doubt, many professional educators were looking to Conant for support again, this time in regard to the education of public-school teachers. Many were disappointed when Conant's criticisms, while more temperate than those of Koerner and others, were in a similar vein.

Conant has sought a balance between liberal and professional studies, but his more basic loyalties to the liberal arts approach and subjects led some of his educationist critics to classify him with those more extreme academicians who have sought to eliminate or diminish professional studies in favor of liberal arts courses. Although he footnoted Conant's more "moderate" orientation, Earle U. Rugg (retired chairman of the division of education at Colorado State College) grouped Conant with Koerner as "status quo seekers" and lamented their neglect of the social aspects of education in favor of the intellectual.[8] Conant's balance is weighted in the direction appropriately termed the "Current Academic Emphasis" in *American Educational Theory* (1964) by Charles J. Brauner, a philosopher of education then at Ohio State University.

Although Conant does not totally ignore the inter-personal and societal aspects of education, he does not stress them, and he is certainly not a "status quo seeker" regarding theory and practice in the education of American teachers. But he speaks for practice and theory, which generally reinforce the present school emphases and the current social order as did the conservative upholders of the life-adjustment ideal. Both of these orientations stand in contrast to the child-centered progressives (William Heard Kilpatrick and young Harold Rugg in the past and A. S. Neill at Summerhill today) who focus on the individual development of the whole child rather than in relation to the pupil's particular talents; the progressive life-adjusters (Harl Douglass and Florence Stratemeyer) who, while not stressing the intellectual, do not especially reduce the two-way process of adjustment to the one-way conformity of life-accommodation; those (Boyd Bode, John Childs, John Dewey, Bruce Raup) who advocated changing the society via the intellectual and personal "reconstruction of experience;" and those (Theodore Brameld, the young George Counts and the later Harold Rugg) who have argued for direct political and social reconstruction on the part of educators. The radical educational view of social reconstructionism has seldom been implemented. When some of the liberal views were in vogue, they were often transformed into conservative and reactionary practices.

Conant is not an academic purist or, to use his term, a separatist. He opposes educationist purism, considering it to be a reaction to academic aloofness. But he has not expressed concern over the fact that his attacks on educationist separatism have given rise in many quarters to a reassertion of academic purism. Many M.A.T. proposals, instead of exemplifying substantial academic-professional cooperation, often require only one or two courses taught in the education department. In the last century, as Merle Borrowman has traced in his book *The Liberal and Technical in Teacher Education* (1956), some educators advocated the professional treatment of subject matter as a fusion which stressed technical competency; others, like Francis Wayland of Brown University, emphasized civic leadership as a proper focus for an integrated teacher education program concentrating on the liberal or general education of teachers. Such a broad vision of teacher education and the teacher role could blend both academic and professional aspects, but it would probably only serve the children well if specific teaching techniques and methods were also included.

Concern for the person as person, not merely as potential teacher, would have to permeate any such integration if it were to be liberal as well as professional. Conant and Dewey have shared the belief that a truly useful education will be liberal and that a liberal education is useful, but Dewey thought that in the perfect program, the conflict would be resolved. Conant sees the dichotomy as a real one that cannot be avoided by an ideal blending but must be faced in each specific working situation. Conant would probably maintain that such a fusion falsely abets basing education on a theoretical model rather than developing it in response to concrete societal, community, and institutional conditions. Here scientific realism seems to enter again. He does not see how any single, unified, ideal plan will solve the constant need to reexamine the claims of all academic or professional interests for possible inclusion in the general or specialized requirements of each particular institution. The organizational structure of colleges and universities continues to require dividing a student's time into academic and professional courses. Campus battles over how much of each should be studied will not subside because curriculum helps determine the areas in which there will be faculty expansion and power. Too frequently, political factors outweigh more liberal considerations.

Unlike Professor Florence Stratemeyer whom Merle Borrowman described in *Teacher Education in America: A Documentary History* (1965) as the present-day standard bearer of the Deweyan integrationist position, Conant seems to fit in Borrowman's nonpurist and nonintegrationist category: the "eclectic or ad hoc" position on the relationship of the liberal and the professional in teacher education. Conant opposes not only the marriage of those components but also their complete separation. He has stated that the general or liberal education of a teacher should not be determined entirely independently of his vocational goals. But as one philosopher of education, Harry S. Broudy of the University of Illinois, has noted among his exceptions to *The Education*, this approach can also lead to diluting a teacher's liberal education.

By his "all-university approach," Conant meant that the total university would somehow, by administrative or faculty committee or interdepartmental action, be actively responsible for the education of teachers. In effect, it was a continuation of his earlier pleas for greater involvement by academic professors. Some professional educators welcome this. Given the historical quarrels and university power struggles, a number still fear it. One problem is that most academic professors properly have other concerns. Their involvement with teacher education is frequently a tangential one. It may merely be misused to support their primary interests.

Paul Woodring has pointed out that the "all-university approach" works when university powers support teacher education. It fails when they do not and when it becomes mainly a ruse to limit the influence and power of educationists. Cooperation among academic and professional educators can produce benefits for the field and for both groups, as well as their colleges and universities. There is a need to recognize competencies of individuals and then seek improvement of the total preparation of American teachers rather than merely the strengthening of one group's institutional position. Greater appreciation is needed by each group for what the other has to contribute. A problem of implementation also arises in those schools where the climate for agreement among academicians and educationists is poor. True cooperation seems most needed where it is least likely to result. Where educationists and academicians value each other's contributions, formal cooperation may still be necessary, but it is less needed.

Journalists were first to react to The Education. The popular press saw the report as front page news because of both author and subject matter. Lead reviews occurred in The New York Times and many other newspapers. Articles or editorials appeared in Life, Time, America, New Yorker, Newsweek, U.S. News and World Report and Reader's Digest, among others. This publicity helped the volume to become a best seller, especially for a book on education. By August of 1965, about 55,000 copies of the hardcover or enlarged paperback edition had been sold. This does not include 5,000 copies of the complimentary edition which had been mailed. The work's popular success made it incumbent upon the profession to grapple with Conant's proposals.

Educators responded later to the book, but more critically and more defensively than the journalists. For the educators, reviewing the book was an additional rather than a prime assignment. They were also more aware of the intricacies of the field and needed more time to assess the details of Conant's recommendations and suggestions. The wave of attacks and criticisms of educationists during and following the McCarthy period contributed to their defensiveness. This might be interpreted as signifying a professional esprit de corps, but not the type Conant once favored being developed among professional educators. Every field has its leaders and its main organizations which might be dubbed its "establishment." Conant's use of that term in the report reinforced the defensiveness of the professionals. While it may have provoked reaction, it also contributed to increasing the rigidity about which Conant complained.

Educationists ought to be highly sensitive to the distance between education's high ideals and its actual conduct. Yet, when put on the defensive by outside criticism, they tend to laud current practices as though their lofty goals were under attack. As Raymond Callahan detailed in *Education and the Cult of Efficiency* (1962), prior to their increased twentieth-century public relations function, educationists (especially administrators) were among the field's severest critics. Maxine Greene indicated in *The Public School and the Private Vision* (1965) that nineteenth-century American educators had a high degree of hope about American life compared to the outlooks of American authors. She thus indirectly supported Conant's general view of educationists as having been utopian optimists. Many educators have attained status and upward social mobility primarily via schooling; writers have generally not succeeded by that formal institutional route. Many school persons tend to have too much faith in the educational system, while some critics, like Evans Clinchy, have expressed little or no faith in the results of school programs with or without government or foundation assistance.

Conant's advocacy of institutional autonomy from "voluntary" accrediting was contrary to the longstanding efforts of many educationists to achieve accreditation for teacher education. Conant's concrete practicalism and aversion to education based on any single theoretical orientation indirectly challenged those who subscribed, consciously or not, to metaphysical or philosophical foundations for the activity of teaching. Conant stated in 1959:

When someone writes or says that what we need today in the United States is to decide first what we mean by the word "education," a sense of distasteful weariness overtakes me. . . . In such a mood, I am ready to define education as what goes on in schools and colleges. I am more inclined to examine the present and past practices of teachers than to attempt to deduce pedagogical concepts from a set of premises. Moreover, the empirical approach has many advantages for an educator concerned with explaining the work of teachers to lay audiences.[9]

But one criticism of Conant's study was that it was not sufficiently empirical.

Attempts to get Conant to speak more directly to the aims of education or schooling, rather than to the

arrangements or means, met with little success. This reinforced the conviction of many educationists that Conant's main goals were less the personal development of
students and more the learning of appropriate societal
content and skills. Of course the two aims are related,
but neither is necessarily defined in terms of the other.
At one 1964 conference, Conant stated that the objective of the all-university approach "is the production of
a man or woman who is well educated as he can be in
every respect as a human being for all purposes in this
society for the purpose of teaching his particular subject." [10] This is one of Conant's few statements on objectives, poorly worded and utopian as it may seem.

Conant is in accord with recent questioning of the
dualism of liberal and professional studies, and the logical and the psychological aspects of education, but he
leans to the first category in each set. He also sympa-
thizes with the current focus on the instructional aspects of teacher behavior. This is in clear contrast to the
earlier endeavors of progressives to expand the teacher's
role from an intellectual one into wider social and psychological guidance. They thus hoped to implement
their developmental and reform aspirations. Conant de-
emphasizes the psychological approach that might
actually increase the instructional effectiveness of
schools. He remains traditionally loyal to subject matter
over a sociopsychological orientation.

The current outlook seems more relevant to the
later rather than the earlier stages of schooling. It reflects the reassertion of concern with preparation for
the reality of adulthood in contrast to the progressive
stress on the present stage of development of the
learner. A combination of concern with the "ladder"
and the present could be more effective and desirable

than either alone. Insofar as the first emphasis takes its clues about the future in terms of the present, it concentrates on the prevailing realities, which are expected to continue and accelerate; by focusing on these conditions and trends as inevitable, it can help to sustain them. If interwoven with concern for developing both creative and critical persons, this approach need not perpetuate the status quo. Without attention to creativity and criticalness in the developmental orientation, mere cultural induction occurs as readily as with a simple subject matter transmission approach. Partisans of both the subject matter and the human development schools of educational thought have too long made strawman targets of each other for the conservatism possible within both orientations.

Combining the subject matter and developmental approaches in their liberating senses would not only facilitate increased mastery of present learning as the best preparation for the future, but would also realize the importance of the intellectual, the creative, the evaluative, and human development in a rapidly changing technological society. The "ladder" or "existential" or combination approach could be used by either academic subject matter or developmental partisans. James Conant could learn from an Edgar Z. Friedenberg or a Paul Goodman or a Harold Taylor and they from him, precisely because their concerns are so diverse. Those whom Peter Schrag has identified as "Education's 'Romantic' Critics" (*Saturday Review*, February 18, 1967) serve a valuable humanistic function when realism reigns, just as realist critics do when idealism is in vogue. A new kind of realism is emerging from disillusionment with wars fought for democracy's sake. Teacher behavior and curriculum structure were ig-

nored when the stress was on child growth and development in relation to the processes of learning. Must we
now neglect the latter factors while emphasizing the
former?

Can we not hold to standards of achievement and
also foster increased skills and knowledge as well as acceptance of the person and by the person of his actual
level of functioning? Must high ideals lead to rejection
of the person's current performance? Can we not praise
positive efforts while accepting their distance from perfection? There is need for both upholding standards
and facilitating effective healthy educational growth.
Standards need to be defined not merely in academic or
personal characteristics, but both. *The Education*
tapped response on one side of these issues (witness
Harold Taylor) because Conant stressed the other side.
Children deserve the combination of academic, personal, and social concerns. Teacher education must
somehow incorporate these aspects.

One of the disappointing results of the controversy
was the small number of academicians who responded
to Conant's criticisms of them. On one hand, this could
indicate that they were not yet ready for an effective
"all-university approach." Few have actually ever experienced it. *The Education* received more published
attention from the literate public than from educationists, but more from educationists than from academicians. As Borrowman suggests in chapter 6, they may
have viewed Conant's charges against them as inserted
merely to balance his criticisms of the educationists. On
the other hand, there has been increasing cooperation
in some institutions among academic and education
professors in both the study of education and the training of teachers. For those who have been so involved,

Conant's plea to end the quarrel is as much an issue of the past as was his stress on multipurpose institutions.

Another disappointing result of *The Education* to Conant supporters was how few college and university presidents championed Conant's request for greater institutional autonomy. His opposition to state course requirements and professional accreditation stems from his concern that these limit the freedom of each higher educational institution to operate without considerable interference from either special-interest groups or public agencies. Some administrators may feel more comfortable with outside groups dictating many decisions rather than assuming the responsibility themselves in addition to mediating related conflicts among the faculty and, now, students. The administrators may also welcome outside support by professionals or the public if it happens to agree with their philosophy or aid its implementation.

Some still believe incorrectly that academic courses are strictly content affairs without process and that education courses are purely methods work without content. One of Conant's many valuable efforts has been to try to bring content and methods closer together. The confusion about academic versus education courses is heightened because many academic courses really have professional goals and some education ones are for liberal purposes. Teachers and their students would gain not only from the increased application of academic disciplines to the study of education, such as Conant recommends, but also from the study of education as a social science in the curriculum of their general education. All students would then directly examine and consider both empirical and theoretical research on the actual operations of educational agencies, institutions, processes, thought, and trends just as they presently do in regard to political, social, and economic systems. Education as a field of inquiry and study could develop the sufficiently agreed-upon content, structure, and rigor to become recognized as a discipline. The liberal aspects of the study of education might even become apparent. Methods teachers could be more concerned with the search for truth and thus be more intellectually challenging. Academicians could be more concerned about the functionality of their courses in terms of both their personal and social rewards and their vocational relevance.

Conant was criticized for using introductory texts and courses as his basis for judging whether or not education was a discipline. Richard Seckinger, education historian at the University of Pittsburgh, reprimanded him for not considering education as a discipline in its own right, and for not distinguishing between a discipline and a science. In *The Discipline of Education* (1963), edited by John Walton and James L. Kuethe of the University of Wisconsin, it was concluded that education was not a discipline because it did not have its own clearly defined content and research methods. The question might be raised whether economics or political science or sociology have a clearly defined content or distinctive research methods in contrast to general social science ones. Conferring the label of discipline on an area of study may be merely a matter of status. People in different disciplines do not always concur as to what makes for a discipline; there is no consensus in the academic world on what comprises a discipline.

Just as there have been earlier and more recent attempts to construct a science of education, as indirectly propounded by Benjamin Bloom and David S. Krathwohl in their two-volume *Taxonomy of Educational Objectives* (1954, 1956) that treats first the cognitive and then the affective domains, there have also been contemporary efforts to define the discipline of education as was done by Marc Belth in his *Education as a Discipline: A Study of the Role of Models in Thinking* (1965). Such endeavors have also focused on teacher goals and behavior, learning processes, the problems of education, and empirical and theoretical research on subjects like the structure of knowledge.

More direct attention to educational matters is needed by generalists and specialists trained in related fields of study as well as by those trained in professional education. Conant's neglect of the latter heightened the controversy by threatening those professional educators who believe that training in both education and a related academic field is necessary for the intermediary professors, whether dually appointed or not. In its 1959 joint report with the Philosophy of Education Society, the committee of philosophy in education of the American Philosophical Association concluded that the philosophy of education instructor "should have a doctorate-level competency in philosophy" *and* "the professional fields of educational study and research," by which it meant "possession of an earned Doctor's degree with a major in philosophy or with a major in philosophy of education from a recognized department of philosophy or of philosophy of education." The Committee realized that "the range of specialization within professional education is too broad to permit a mastery of every area," but it recommended that the background of the philosopher in education should include "history of education, sociological and political backgrounds, the psychology of human learning and development." [11]

In focusing on the practical art of teaching and the desirability of experienced teachers having contact with academic men whose prime or sole interests are in education, Conant does not appear to consider the study of education essential to the preparation of teachers. Nor does he desire that intermediary professors be trained in other than one academic discipline. He has long sided with depth and specialization. His minimal recommendations for prospective teachers also remain mainly straight academics plus supervised teaching, although his suggestions are broader.

In their book *Education and the New America* (1962), Solon T. Kimball and James E. McClellan, Jr. suggested that the progressive education movement was an effort to retain agrarian ideals in a corporate industrial society. Of Conant, they wrote: "Nor are we likely to find an intelligible rationale for our rapidly growing school system in James Conant's many writings on education. Mr. Conant, as a matter of fact, deliberately rejects the idea that our schools actively need any rationales other than their ongoing, immediate objectives." [12] But Conant's attempt to have teaching ideals defined situationally might be perceived as a decentralized and apparently nonideological approach to developing goals for a technological rather than an agrarian society. Whether this is adequate for our society is debatable. One of Conant's own pleas is that there be a nationwide educational policy resulting from interstate cooperation. A seemingly less ideological orientation appears to suit a "how-minded" technological society and to service heterogeneity, but it may also diminish rather than foster pluralism. Professor Thomas Green developed the latter point in his 1966 Syracuse University J. Richard Street Lecture entitled "Education and Pluralism: Ideal and Reality." Perhaps Professor M.I. Berger of the State University of New York at Albany sensed that when he complained about Conant's lack of existentialism, mentioned earlier in this chapter, when he referred to Conant's "Yankee liberalism."

Conant's educational philosophy stresses the individual person less than the philosophy of the early progressives did. It exhibits more of the care about the system and the society than we find in the later progressives. Conant is distinguished from the progressives by his concern with fostering the workability of the American socioeconomic system rather than altering it. Kimball and McClellan view change of the system as needed to assist its workability. All three agree upon promoting complete equality of opportunity for all as a necessary social commitment. Conant's focus is on the importance of talent to the technocracy if the free society is to survive the long range cold war and the short range limited ones.

In *The Community of Scholars* (1962), Paul Goodman argues that "philosophers of education" Conant and Jefferson really differ basically "because their national goals are different." Goodman quotes Conant twice (both times inaccurately in words, but correctly in substance) to the effect that Conant admits that liberal arts professors often discuss school matters as though the schools existed in a social vacuum, and that some administrators and teachers are so tied to their concern for "the unfolding of the individuality of each child that they automatically resist any idea that a new national concern might be an important factor. . . ." Goodman states that the crucial factor is what the national goals are, and that:

The bother with these remarks of Dr. Conant is that he himself discusses the "national needs" as if they existed in a social, and human, vacuum. But in his four books on the schools—prepared on a grant from the Carnegie Corporation—he is in fact seeking to mold education merely to bail out an overmature, overcentralized, venal, and conformist status quo in the final epoch of the national states: hurriedly to train "scientists" to wage the Cold War, to man the existing and monstrously growing corporations with apprentices and technicians, and to dampen the "social dynamite," as he calls it, of unemployment in the city slums. These national needs he never questions, but he often expresses his impatience with philosophers of education.

Jefferson, however, was concerned with building a new nation by means of a society as open, as unadministered, and as international as he could strategize. These were the national needs.[13]

The progressives have shared Conant's emphasis on a high degree of social mobility, but much less his concern with social stability. Many progressives were also more prone to subscribe to a particular metaphysics (pragmatism) to further their aims than Conant seems to be. But the progressives were less tied than Conant to a specific political, economic, and social order. These matters divided the progressives among themselves and from the general public. The progressives were more in accord with the war and prewar atmosphere in which, to use Max Lerner's phrase, *Ideas Are Weapons* (1939). Conant appears closer to the newer climate described by Daniel Bell as *The End of Ideology* (1960); as a realist, Conant discourages emphasis on any associations between his "discoveries" and his "personal" social ideology.

After labeling Dr. Conant an empiricist in *Formative Ideas in American Education* (1965), V. T. Thayer expressed his view that Conant is not without an outlook. Neither are Kimball and McClellan. All three attempt to base their beliefs on their analyses of social conditions rather than on a priori metaphysics. But their realism is of two different types. Kimball and McClellan stress the teaching of adequate skills and loyalties to improve an individual's realization in a corporate society; Conant emphasized the development of individual abilities to keep the system functioning well. Both the individual and the social focuses are necessary. In this "Age of the Mass Culture" (to quote Willis Rudy again), the former seems more neglected in practice. The transition from an emphasis on the individual to society was partly a reaction by the later progressives to the Depression, industrialism, and the wars that have characterized contemporary American society.

Conant's moderate positions match the social climate of the sixties in contrast to the post-Depression period. His realist nonideological orientation fits the social atmosphere that has contributed to the death of progressive education as a social movement and which has also fostered the acceptance of limited, fighting wars and psychological warfare, as opposed to all-out, hot wars. Realism, whether Conant's or Kimball's or McClellan's, encourages facing those specific conditions which are expected to persist and increase. It thus supports recognition of and in a certain sense, maintenance of the accepted facts and trends of contemporary life. Inevitably, adults must confront these as the realities, desirable or not, with which they must live.

This is not a time when immense changes in the social machinery can be anticipated even if they are needed. It is an age of caution and care, of a new awareness of the real complexities of the world, and of increased suspicion of easy answers to difficult questions. Conant's hopeful realism, while dampening the vast social reform aspirations characteristic of most great educators of the past, has widespread popular appeal to a society devoted to survival and to preserving and promoting its basic worth more than questioning or evaluating it. Protest movements, whether of an economic or black power or peace variety, seem to be growing; but they presently exist as semitolerated minority expressions just as do educational patterns stressing student freedom and election, and independent, self-directed study.

While the progressives strove to reform society by reconstructing education, Conant seeks to increase social mobility but conserve essential American social patterns through altering education in line with new technological conditions. He sees his Jeffersonianism, with its emphasis on educating for a leadership "meritocracy" (to use Michael Young's phrase from *The Age of Meritocracy*), as necessary and suited to today's world. Others like Cremin and John W. Gardner seem to concur with Conant on this. There have been no major dissenters regarding this contemporary need for leadership.

The progressives also favored the development of leaders, but generally conceived of them more as intellectual and social critics (as many progressives have been) than as politically-effective compromisers like Conant. The progressives were more idealistic social scientists and philosophers than realist social engineers and managers. The progressives were conforming with their conception of the American ideal—social improvement to expand freedom and individuality. Societal development for individual or personal growth (or the reverse) has always been the liberal creed.

Conant conceives his administrative role as that of weaving together the diverse elements of tradition. He seeks the continuity of the social order, which he views as providing sufficient freedom; the progressives want that freedom greatly extended. Conant does desire expansion of society's benefits to greater numbers of people, but he is cautious about how much can be done, and how quickly, without upsetting the system. He is especially concerned about the increased role of the federal government. While favoring racial equality, he has been reluctant to support what appear to him as radical means of securing racial balance and integration, such as the bussing of children. As perceived by this writer, societal evolution appears to require periods of consolidation between times of marked alteration. If Conant's proposals represent a revolution, it is a socially conservative one with both positive and negative aspects.

His Jeffersonian concern with societal leadership and his advocacy of ability-grouping in some subjects and levels contrasts sharply with the Jacksonian progressives' emphasis on heterogeneous "classless" mixing of youth of different abilities and social backgrounds. Robert Havighurst and Bernice Neugarten's summary of studies in *Society and Education* (1967) indicates a high positive correlation between tested ability and social background in general, possibly due to hereditary and environmental factors as well as class-biased means of measuring talent. Whether ability-grouping fosters or hinders social mobility is still controversial.

Conant's Jeffersonian realism places greater faith in factors other than school instruction as influences on the potential and performance of youth. In contrast, as documented in Henry J. Perkinson's *The Imperfect Panacea: American Faith in Education, 1865–1965* (1968), many Jacksonians have had a seemingly religious faith in what they can accomplish in the schools. Such faith may be necessary to stimulate the extra effort many educational goals require given limited available resources. When Jacksonians have lacked confidence in just how much schools can do, they have adopted the wider concept of education as the total socialization process involving all societal educational agencies such as family peer-group, mass media, church, library, youth organizations, and others. Conant, like Cremin, has recognized this wider concept of education in terms of a community and social process and has asked for studies of education in this broader context. To the disappointment of many, Conant's teacher education study (unlike parts of some of his other education works) was not of that dimension.

Conant's aversion to the attempts of educators to reshape the society via the schools seems related to his dread of what this approach has meant and still means in totalitarian nations. In a recent *Phi Delta Kappan* article, George S. Counts stated that his famous and controversial 1937 pamphlet *Dare the Schools Build a New Social Order?* was being enacted in the "Great Society" program, but my thesis is that the "Great Society" is mostly concerned with a broader dispersal of the benefits of the present economic, political, and social systems rather than any basic change in them. The only way this writer sees schools possibly serving as agents of social reconstruction is indirectly, as Boyd Bode indicated years ago, by fostering intellectual and personal "reconstruction of experience." Only a minority of teachers and leaders is achieving that goal. For school systems and individual teachers to be direct agents of social change, they require the backing of those in power. These leaders are in control by virtue of political, social, and economic endorsements already secured. They are therefore most apt to support the status quo and to sanction only those changes already approved by the politically active and powerful—but this is democracy in action. This is probably the reason that many leaders like Stephen Bailey of the Syracuse University Maxwell School of Social Science, have urged teachers to become more politically astute, active, and effective in the making of educational policy.

Conant seeks to combine educating for leadership with educating the common man. In this vein, he ended his series of 1952 talks on *Education and Liberty*:

For the future we must endeavor to combine the British concern for training the "natural aristocracy of talents" with the American insistence on general education for *all* future citizens. If we can do that, then our industrialized society will prosper and at the same time the necessary degree of instruction will be provided for all the people so that in their hands "our liberties will remain secure." [14]

Conant has previously advocated his Jeffersonianism in combination with Jacksonianism. As early as 1938, he wrote:

Those of us who are confident of the continued triumph of democracy can have no fear lest the Jacksonian tradition of education for all perish. But in regard to the Jeffersonian tradition we may feel more apprehension, for it has never taken deep root even in this country, its native land. We must continually urge upon the nation the desirability of directing the expenditure of public money for education with the selective process in mind.[15]

As Conant recognizes, Jeffersonianism emerged in the 1960's as a more acceptable viewpoint in a corporate, technological society involved in both cold wars and limited, fighting ones. A stress on educating the talented is seldom branded undemocratic today. The current need may be for more Jacksonianism to accompany rather than to supplant the new and necessary concerns with ability and excellence. In fact, *Excellence* is the title of a 1961 education bestseller by John W. Gardner. His subtitle evidences his own subscription to the combination: "Can We Be Equal and Excellent Too?" Gardner's *Self-Renewal* (1963) referred to both the individual and the innovative society. In his 1965 annual report of the Carnegie Corporation of New York, Gardner asked that universities become more concerned with training for moral and societal leadership, rather than merely preparing intellectual experts; but he also sought more specialized leaders who could communicate more effectively with each other.

Alfred North Whitehead's idea of the bipolarity of conflicting but complementary concepts suggests one possibility of combining Jacksonianism and Jeffersonianism. His construct explains that while there is conflict and competition between the two orientations, they are also mutually dependent and reinforce one another, just as do breadth and depth in learning. Whitehead's views are generally gaining a greater hearing in our age of moderation, and there seems to be some movement towards a Jacksonian-Jeffersonian blend. Conant, Cremin and Gardner have stressed as true Jeffersonianism the combination of egalitarianism and standards which is, in Cremin's book-title, *The Genius of American Education* (1966). In that book, Cremin noted:

Dewey, too, saw himself as a Jeffersonian, though he spent a good part of his life seeking to resolve certain dualisms that were at the very heart of the Jeffersonian view. . . . But instead of following Mann in stressing the equalitarian aspects of Jefferson's program as against the elitist, Dewey recast the alternatives in a formulation so radical we have yet to apply it.[16]

Cremin points out that Dewey sought no qualitative difference between the education of the public and that of its leaders. This is in contrast to Conant who wants some differentiation of students in varied curricula within a comprehensive institutional organization and who in his *Slums and Suburbs* (1961), urged special vocational courses for those with below average abilities. The equalitarian Jeffersonians stress caution in judging or assuming potential on the basis of performance. They are also concerned with those out-of-school environmental social-psychological conditions that influence the development and talent of individual students. Cremin also urged the public to be more alert to the narcotic effects of the commercial mass media. Conant has not totally ignored nonschool educational agencies but he has concentrated heavily on schools rather than on outside, and sometimes more influential, educational and formative institutions.

Whether under the dual Jacksonian-Jeffersonian label or the single Jeffersonian one Cremin employs, the synthesis maintains the aim of a highly educated leadership need not be opposed to that of a well-educated public. Despite its historical authenticity, one problem with the single Jeffersonian term is that many, like Foerster, Mueller, or Nock, have not included its equalitarian aspects while others, like Conant, emphasize under it the selectivity and education for leadership portion more than the expansionist, Jacksonian concerns. Restressing one of Thomas Green's points mentioned in the first chapter of this book, and now in print in his *Work, Leisure, and the American Schools* (1968): Emphasis on selectivity in schools also perverts guidance to the functions of testing and tracking the students rather than increasing their self-awareness and aiding in their development of self-identity. There is little doubt that American society needs to be greatly concerned with developing its leaders, but (as Conant and Gardner know) Jefferson also wrote in contrasting America to Europe that one of the most dangerous social conditions is to have the few highly educated and the vast majority much less educated.

We can produce leaders in the process of educating each and every individual not merely to the best of the learner's ability, but also to the best of the educators' ability. This lofty goal is still the overall challenge to education in a free society with allegiances to universal schooling. Education for leadership must be of all types and part of the education of all. Talent, ability, potential, and capacity are still inferred from all that we ever really know—actual performance. By merely recognizing and encouraging what we call ability or talent, we are not necessarily producing it. Except in extreme cases, we must realize that we do not know if low-level performance is the result of lack of ability or simply inadequate nurturing and training. New programs may well show it is mostly the latter; and that poor performance has been too frequently dismissed as unalterable lack of talent by those without the knowledge, skills or desire to improve such performance. For the emotionally disturbed, the methods may be strictly psychiatric or psychological. In the extreme case of retarded children, the methods may even be chemical. Despite all kinds of dogmatic proclamations, we do not know for sure the relative impact of genetics and early environment on intelligence. Pragmatists dismiss this question too easily with their reductionist answer of "it's both." When differences in degree become significant, they make for differences in kind. Assuming that there is differential ability from variable performance leads to a completely different educational system than when this is not presumed.

Promoting social mobility among lower classes must be accompanied by a realistic assessment of working-class life, not merely a rejection of it and indirectly of the worker himself. Gordon Allport documented in *The Nature of Prejudice* (1954) that more prejudice exists among those who have been socially mobile (up or down, although more if down) than among those persons who have remained in the social milieu in which they were born. When the features (positive and negative) of lower-class life are faced, the learning situation is more realistic and better suited to the acquiring of skills necessary to a rise in social class. To educate for upward social mobility necessitates teaching middle-class customs to the poor, but these are often foreign to their primary experiences and difficult to learn. For educators to overlook either of the horns of this dilemma will mean failure just as does refusing to face limiting obstacles or confronting them without hope they can be overcome.

The similarities between lower-class and middle-class life need to be stressed, not merely the differences. Deprivation and disadvantage ought to be defined not only in terms of poverty and social mobility but also in psychological terms. The defects of middle-class American life, as exhibited in excessive status-seeking, need to be considered. It is not only lower-class American life which needs reevaluation and reconstruction. Conant's achievement-oriented upward mobility striving system ought not be the only school-approved cultural pattern. Students should be encouraged to assess the values and problems of both mobility and stability and of future achievement personality patterns with existentially present affiliation ones. For many economically-deprived youths, social mobility does not seem a real enough goal for which to strive; just staying employed may be a struggle. For many middle-class children, upward mobility striving is the only life-style they know.

For education to enrich individual lives, full appreciation of one's actual position in society needs to be combined with healthy striving. This might mean the individual electing to pursue social mobility or not in terms of his own efforts at self-actualization or, in Victor Frankl's term, self-transcendence. Schools need to promote self-realization which may mean either stability or mobility. For the vast majority of people, the opportunity for self-realization is linked to upward social mobility. In the past, Conant has stressed upward social mobility for the more talented of the lower classes, and less striving for the less talented of the upper-status groups.

In accepting a predetermined ability limit as did Plato and Jefferson, Conant opposes striving beyond one's actual capacities; but he feels the system has neglected the bright child whom he wants guided toward greater accomplishment. How natural capacity is determined is not clear. Conant thinks that the kind and amount of talent in the individual are the essential factors in determining potential rather than learned interests or motivation. The social class and the sex of the individual affect his kind and amount of measured ability as well as his interests and motivation. The bases of choice must be left to the person; but hopefully, teachers and guidance counselors will serve students by helping them to make such decisions with increased awareness of their own possibilities and of the socio-cultural influences. Striving for success should always be encouraged when success is defined in many unique ways by the persons involved, not merely by school officials and society. Only in this way can individuality be fostered.

II THE NEED FOR BALANCE AND A SYNTHESIS

If one avoids immersion in the specific issues of the Conant controversy and instead surveys the general conflict of orientations, more than the Jeffersonian and Jacksonian strains appear. Those who differed with Conant's selection of basic issues emphasized generalist, societal, existential, human, personal, interpersonal, developmental, psychological, emotional, and attitudinal factors in education as contrasted to his specialist, academic, factual, structural, organizational, content, logical and concretist, societal, administrative emphasis. His theses elicited the antitheses. In *The Freeing of Intelligence Through Teaching* (1961), Gardner Murphy has suggested that love between teachers and students involves a common search for reality requiring generalists and specialists, and a dialectic among the personalists and the rationalists in education. While the Conant controversy never quite developed into such a dialectic, the elements were there. As Conant tended to stress rationalist factors, many like Harold Taylor responded with personalist ones.

Both rationalists and personalists can gain from greater concern with the factors which seem more important to the other. A balance and a synthesis are needed. The process of education consists of personal (physical, psychological, and emotional) and social, as well as academic intellectual and vocational variables. Overemphasis or neglect of any of these factors can skew the content-process relationship and limit education's effectiveness. Some teachers need more stress on the rationalist factors; some, on the personalist ones. We need to blend concerns with an individual and his growth with our national needs. Intellectual competency should be viewed as an important part of development, though not the only one. To emphasize product in education and neglect process may arise from a technological orientation, but it makes as little sense as stressing process without concern for product. The first seems the greater danger today, because the materialistic benefits of the technological culture are the goals for which most people in our society learn to strive. Those who achieve them might then get concerned with something more. Materialism is to be supported in the hope that it may become a means to attaining more humanistic goals. The problem is that this materialistic seeking can become an end in itself, transforming man into the means.

The question of how theory and practice should be related is not new to the fields of education and philosophy. Theory has been viewed traditionally by philosophers as the firm foundation upon which practice ought to be based, because theory has been considered superior when it was prior to and most removed from practical consideration. Pragmatists argued instead that the ultimate test of a theory lies in its practical use. They emphasized the operational consequences of an idea. By stressing the fruits of both the deductive and inductive modes in science, Conant has indirectly asserted that the relationship can be in either direction as in the case of theoretical physics or a practical inventor like Edison. Conant has said he would educate individuals by the deductive or the inductive mode, whichever suited them most; but in the education of teachers, he says he favors the latter approach. In education, his inductive scientific, action-oriented bias appears to outweigh his contemplative reflective side. However, his statements on his choice may actually result from the deductive approach. Education needs both modes.

Conant has maintained that ideally practice and theory should be balanced and go hand in hand, but he has been specially critical of theory preceding practice. He has been explicit about this concern regarding the educational system of Germany and, by his proposals, implicit about it in the United States. His realist educational leanings support student-teaching preceding the study of theory. Some teacher education programs even have methods courses after student-teaching because they are then more relevant to the student's prior experience. One study has shown that there seems to be little difference in student-teaching performance when methods courses precede it, but that there is increased appreciation of methods courses when they are taken after teaching experience.[17]

While the Conant study did not mention it, some institutions provide for student-teaching in the junior rather than the senior year, so students can discover whether teaching is really their career before the end of their undergraduate years. This also has the advantage of placing methods and theory courses both before and after teaching experience. One problem with methods courses *after* student-teaching is that school systems cannot count on as well-prepared student-teachers as in the reverse pattern. However, they can help students to find the ways they prefer, rather than having to discard many "ideal" approaches of teacher education institutions which later prove impractical.

The fears of some educationists that Conant's approach fosters a craft or trade orientation become further understandable in view of Charles J. Brauner's analysis in *American Educational Theory* (1964) of the monitorial system (whereby one teacher taught large numbers of students through student monitors) as an example of practice-centered theory. More controlled empirical studies and more sophisticated analyses are needed of this question: What is the relationship of education theory and practice? Some philosophers of education assert that there is a deductive logical connection between theory and practice; others deny the logical implication but maintain that one's education theories have perceptual and psychological implications for teacher behavior.[18] Conant totally ignores the last possibility in his "practice before theory" position. It may well be that many of the seemingly methodological debates, such as those on the best way to teach reading, result partly from the different reasons for desiring that skill: functional literacy, widening horizons, acquaintance with literature, deepening levels of comprehension, oral pronunciation, improved communication and citizenship. Conant assumes the basic skills and subjects to be taught. He does not discuss how these are best learned or the best methods of teaching them in relation to the different goals sought by different teachers in each area.

Financial pressures and improved technological equipment like computers, television, and teaching machines are accentuating certain direct instructional modes of teaching. Like the monitorial and teacher-aide systems, these new media appear to decrease the need for personal teacher-student contact. Sometimes, this seems to be to the student's advantage, as in O.K. Moore's talking typewriters used to teach reading. Educational technology can also serve to free teachers for more direct personal and social approaches. How the new technology is to be used is a crucial matter. Educators can reflect and contribute to the role-compartmentalization of corporate times. But as much as they might try to continue agrarian ideals of integrity and social relatedness rather than urban alienation, educators cannot revive agrarianism as a way of life. Nor was the "Home on the Range" as rosy as some selective memories recall it.

With the use of time-saving machines, teachers could treat the individual more as an end than as a means, but to do this properly, most need more psychological and sociological depth than they presently possess. Conant's approach to professional studies in teacher education increases a mechanistic and methodological orientation and decreases the sociological and psychological emphasis because his concern with content is mainly in terms of its transmission.

The dangers of an approach to education that is merely mechanistic and technological became apparent to this writer when he was the first to try a computer-assisted course in history of education at an institution he was visiting. The machine told him he was wrong in naming the Massachusetts School Law of 1647 the "Satan Deluder Act" because it was the "Old Satan Deluder Law." The machines will be only as good as those who program them. If a "seed-catalog" approach to history is that of the programmer, the machine will not aid in promoting a liberal education any more than would that same instructor without the machine. The human factor remains decisive. Machines may, in fact, have an even greater impact than direct human teaching because they present human-designed material to the learner as though it were strictly impersonal. The content then appears more infallible than it really is. Like atomic energy, our technological improvements are only advances when used to benefit and free man rather than to destroy, limit, and imprison his magnificent, potential powers of creativity.

The heightened interest in the Montessori system, which stresses the student learning directly and "inductively" from preset materials and equipment, also seems related to the impersonal, complex, urban corporate setting with more diffuse bureaucratic structures and less directly responsible authorities. The discovery approach to teaching is often used to lead students to "discover" what it is predetermined they are supposed to find. Just as with the life-adjustment or the community-school ideal, liberal educational approaches can become perverted to serving conservative societal goals. Even the nongraded school which was developed to educate each pupil more individually is sometimes just a mask for homogeneous ability grouping, which may or may not incorporate individualization of instruction.

When preceded by practical experience, the study of educational theory can refer to the practical classroom problems the student has already encountered. But the facing of the latter would have been done without prior study of alternatives. Each teacher, then, is solely responsible for his own decisions, made without reliance on previous formal study of the thoughts of others on such matters. This can increase dependency on the current system and be a way of reinforcing it. Teaching behavior will then probably neglect significant value variables and philosophical alternatives not previously delineated. This is especially likely because philosophy courses are now so seldom required even in general or liberal education. Conant probably opposes theory before practice because the former has too often been even more prescriptive than are the dictates of actual conditions.

Teachers are frequently unclear as to why they are teaching their subject or how their own goals are related to what their students hope to learn. Frequently, teachers merely follow prescribed curriculum. This is particularly so in New York where many teachers say the Regents' examinations determine what they must teach. There is some truth to this. Like texts, curriculum guides can become crutches for avoiding responsible choices or they can serve as valuable teacher aids. When teaching is fully a profession, like medicine, individual teachers will select their own materials (in coordination with other teachers and perhaps their students). They will not be legislated or "guided" into covering societally safe topics, and then absolved of their personal and professional responsibilities for following possibly undesirable prescribed paths. If teachers are not individually responsible for what they teach, it seems folly to expect students who are given even less choice, to accept responsibility for what they learn.

In teaching undergraduate education courses, this writer has been surprised that despite all prior theoretical emphasis on individual differences, student-teachers would react with amazement at the great variation among pupils. While this might support Conant's stress on practice before theory, it is also possible that the students' recognition of these differences was heightened by the antecedent cognitive learning. While much more empirical and theoretical research is needed on this, the necessity to make teacher education more realistic became evident to me when even some of my older adult students who had been preparing to teach would announce to me one to two years after their graduation that, to their surprise, they were really teaching. Conant shows his awareness that a long theoretical preparatory period can reduce its apparent relevancy.

The interrelatedness of theory and practice may hold, but when people act regardless of awareness or previous thought, they may rationalize their behavior rather than evaluate it critically. An education program for student-teachers just starting to teach that highlights variables judged important by experienced teachers might be more effective and more stimulating at that time than later. This could, on the other hand, be stifling, depending, as usual, on the teacher. The danger of merely inducting new teachers into old patterns exists in any approach. Identifying and weighing important problems and alternatives seem more consequential functions than the matter of success or failure at attaining final solutions. This process would also enable prospective teachers to consider techniques of reforming both practices and institutions so the teacher would not be at the mercy of tradition in the actual job situation.

One approach might be discussion seminars emphasizing the students' anticipated problems and assessing of alternative solutions. An expert discussion leader could help by referring to empirical studies, by explaining the different theoretical concepts, and by delineating and clarifying additional possibilities. Fostering evaluation of innovations and ways of implementing the desirable ones could well be a major focus of the theoretical and practical aspects of teacher education. Having "teacher catalysts" who are free to help release the creative energies of those teachers who seem to possess them is one new idea some public schools are trying. This is an example of the educative role of the administrator whether in public schools or teacher education, but too many clerical duties, the demands of higher authorities, and the intellectual limitations of many administrators often prevent them from fulfilling that function.

Philosopher of education George Newsome, Jr. has written, "theoretical knowledge is no guarantee of practical skills," but it "is likely to give one new insights into old problems, or perhaps enables one to better perceive new problems." [19] The relationships between conceptions and perceptions have significant implications for teaching and teacher education. Until more is known about that, one temporary solution may lie in more extensive application in teacher education of the directed case-study approach. Conant has advocated this in the education of lawyers and businessmen. It could be done by case studies, films, tapes, and observations prior to practice teaching. The case-study method could be very useful for bringing out relevant factors if the cases tap basic issues and if they are truly open-ended and are not rigged for the correct solutions. Sarason, Davidson, and Blatt in *The Preparation of Teachers: An Unstudied Problem in Education* (1962) have also urged that teachers be trained in observing teaching situations so that they can be attuned to the actual, and often subtle, behavior and interaction that takes place in the classroom. Campus schools with observation rooms and one-way screens can aid here as can simulated taped classrooms which require a prospective teacher to react and then undergo an evaluation of his teaching actions.

Students in teacher education need not be required to have certain specific state-required courses, the current practice which Conant also opposes. Colleges and universities could develop a variety of teacher education programs. Through accreditation, students could still be expected to have some kind of competency or learning experience in educational and developmental psychology and in at least one of these subjects or disciplines as applied to education: anthropology, comparative education, economics, geography, history, philosophy, political science, social psychology, or sociology. Students would gain immensely from association with someone trained in at least one of those academic societal fields who is also sufficiently well educated in professional aspects to apply it and who is concerned enough to do so. As suggested earlier, all students might include at least one such experience as part of their liberal education and prospective teachers at least two.

The competency of these academic professionals

ought to include, in addition to their academic specialty, some study of aspects of education itself and of the application of related disciplines. Such experiences might be attested to in the same way that doctoral tools now are—by examination or testimony. Much more psychology than Conant suggests also seems needed. Should not all high school teachers have one course in adolescent psychology in addition to general and educational psychology? After all, many will be working with youth at that stage for the rest of their careers. The same reasoning could be applied to those who work with early or late childhood, or young or middle-aged adults or the elderly. Would minors in the liberal academic psychological and cultural areas, as related to the theoretical and practical aspects of education, be too much to require somewhere in the undergraduate or graduate preparation of teachers?

Educational research and the "pure" study of the field of education can take place apart from teacher preparation. There is sufficient room in the academic community for such contributions without those scholars necessarily being also involved in the applied task of teacher training. A teacher-education program without any contact with some of these basic disciplines, as applied to the teaching function, seems much less intellectually rewarding than a program where the institution (not necessarily the state) requires such contact, before, during, or after practical experience. Conant has termed such a state requirement "prescribed exposure," but he has not so labeled it when university-mandated. He acknowledges the value of the intermediary professors, but resists any such course requirements by the state, urging that universities require merely educational psychology for elementary teachers.

Conant says he hopes that the more mature teachers will choose such foundation studies after teaching experience. If part of his rationale for advocating election is that the teachers must see the need for these courses in order to profit from them, he should be consistent in desiring more professional electives throughout the education of teachers. In his sponsored *General Education in a Free Society* report, Conant did not delay requiring broad exposure in liberal fields until the student saw the need to elect it, but still he recommends election for professional work. To be totally consistent, Conant might have maintained, as James E. Russell did in respect to college teaching in his *Change and Challenge in American Education* (1965), that practice-teaching should only be mandatory where it is desired by the student or seems definitely necessary.

Conant has argued for concentration in the teaching subjects for both elementary and secondary teachers, but against it in the professional areas. This is probably related to his long-standing belief that concentration in "old-fashioned subjects" represents the best method of selectivity presently available to determine competency prior to performance. The low academic standards of many teacher education programs too readily support his proposals. Educationists frequently need higher academic standards, and academicians more humane ones.

Conant's strong objections to interference with institutional autonomy by state course requirements led some to perceive his proposals as being primarily aimed at weakening the power of the state in the certification of teachers. Conant wants to limit, but strengthen, the role of the state in evaluating the teaching of the graduates of approved institutions, but he does not specify the means for doing it. That would involve the judgment of professional educators more than the public. But as Cremin has noted in *The Genius* . . . , Conant (in contrast to Myron S. Lieberman) has also favored greater public control of educational policy as shown in his interstate compact proposal. He wants the states to approve institutions rather than specific programs. This would also strengthen his university, state college, and community college hierarchical bias. His rationale is that a good institution should be free to develop its own good programs. He has pointed to both New York and California, with two of the strongest state departments of education in the country, as leading the way: "Leaving New York City aside for the moment, I would be prepared to go so far as to say that if one could imagine combining California's master plan for higher education with New York's Board of Regents and its Commissioner of Education, one would have an example of American public education at its best." [20] As Paul Goodman has pointed out, Conant favors standardization of public education, but not of higher education.

In accord with his emphasis on institutional autonomy, Conant directly attacked the National Council for the Accreditation of Teacher Education. Started in 1952, NCATE was not the first organization to accredit teacher education institutions. Standards for accrediting were first adopted in 1923 by the institutional representatives who comprised the American Association of Teachers Colleges. Four years later, AATC began accrediting. In 1948, AATC merged with the National Association of Teacher Education Institutions in Metropolitan Areas and the National Association of Colleges and Departments of Education to form the American Association of Colleges for Teacher Education. AACTE continued the accrediting functions until 1954

when NCATE instituted formal accrediting procedures. Most of the more than a thousand teacher education institutions approved by AACTE had ignored its
accrediting role.

The initial impetus for NCATE came from a 1948
Bowling Green Conference of the National Commission on Teacher Education and Professional Standards
(NCTEPS) of the NEA. It was then decided to call a
national TEPS conference on accrediting. Two years
later, at such a meeting in Indiana, John Dale Russell,
then head of the United States Office of Education's
Division of Higher Education, asked in his keynote address for the establishment of a joint council for accrediting teacher education. He suggested that it broadly
represent teacher education institutions, the organized
teaching profession, and the appropriate state and local
education officials, lay and professional. A temporary
committee of sixteen members with representatives of
AACTE, NCTEPS, the Council of Chief State School
Officers and the National School Boards Association designed NCATE to consist of twenty-one members: six
from AACTE, six appointed by NEA's Executive
Committee (nominated by NCTEPS), six from the
state education authorities (three from the Council of
Chief State School Officers and three from the National
Association of State Directors of Teacher Education
and Certification), and three appointed by the National School Boards Association.

Conant's criticisms of NCATE were not new. Even
with the NCATE reorganization, he considered only
four members to be independent of NEA influence
since he saw AACTE, the organization of institutions
of teacher education, as being mainly an NEA arm. Conant expressed concern about the inadequate represen-

tation of scholarly disciplines and lay representatives. He does not advocate more representation for the directly involved practitioners, as has Myron S. Lieberman.[21] NCATE's Conference of One Hundred, involving representatives from some fifty national organizations and learned societies and coming as it did in November 1963, falsely appeared to be a result of the Conant volume. Plans for that reevaluation predated publication of The Education, but the report increased the attention given the conference.

The Education was a possible factor in the consideration by the conference of a plan whereby three of a twenty-one member council would be selected by a panel consisting of twelve persons picked by the American Council of Learned Societies (college teachers in the languages, literature, philosophy, and the arts), twelve by the American Association for the Advancement of Science (college science and mathematics teachers), and two each by the American Anthropological Association, American Economic Association, American Historical Association, American Political Science Association, American Psychological Association, and American Sociological Association. In contrast to Conant's position, the following NCATE stand was reiterated at that Conference:

The nature of the data available or procurable on the performance of persons who have completed programs of teacher education requires that accreditation be based primarily on those criteria regarded as the best predictors of quality and those measurable insights and skills possessed by students at the time they complete teacher education programs. The Council has not found a dependable way to evaluate the performance of the product.[22]

Yet, if the only effect of Conant's stress on teacher certification based on teaching performance rather than course accumulation was "a dependable way" to assess teaching behavior (as in the U.S. Office of Education project mentioned by Merle Borrowman in Chapter 6), Conant's contribution to education would be enormous.

In a 1965 Report on *Accreditation in Teacher Education* for the National Commission on Accrediting (NCA), John R. Mayor, indicating his survey had begun in December of 1964, devoted a section to the impact of the Conant report. Mayor stated that Conant's arguments against accrediting in teacher education could be applied to all national accrediting associations and that while NCATE's representation possibly was too narrow, it was considered by some to be broader than that of most accrediting agencies in other fields. Mayor pointed out that while some thought limiting accrediting agencies to an advisory role would end their functioning, the critics might welcome that result. He contended that while Conant wanted full freedom for legitimate institutions, he did not specify any action to exclude the diploma mills in the over one-third of the states which lack effective legislation against them. Elsewhere, Conant had spoken for stronger state regulations in that regard.[23] In asking for reciprocity among states in teacher certification but against national accrediting as a means of securing it, Conant opposed the basis used in dentistry, law, and medicine, not merely in teacher education.

The recent criticisms of NCATE derived mainly from a 1960 decision by NCA to review NCATE's structure and operations. Especially publicized became NCATE's evaluation of the University of Wisconsin, which erupted, along with the Carleton College dispute, while Conant was working on *The Education*. The Wisconsin graduate program was fully accredited but NCATE gave provisional status to the undergraduate one. The University of Wisconsin School of Education executive committee challenged NCATE's procedures and standards by withdrawing its application. The popular notion developed that the core of the dispute was the widespread involvement of liberal arts professors in teacher education at the University of Wisconsin. According to the Mayor Report, these were not the explicit NCATE complaints. Dean Lindley J. Stiles' strong support of Conant's teacher education study probably relates to the University of Wisconsin's School of Education difficulties with NCATE.[24]

Mayor concluded in his report that "accreditation has served to stifle, somewhat, innovation and experimentation, often because institutions thought an accrediting agency was less flexible than it actually intended to be," and he recommended broad participation "of all segments in higher education having a responsibility for the education of teachers."[25] In October of 1965, AACTE membership on NCATE was increased from seven to ten, making a total of twenty-two council members. The direction was to increase institutional representatives, and the three-member NCA ad hoc committee was changed to represent "learned societies," selected by a committee with seven of thirteen votes by AACTE institutional representatives.

The most direct effect of *The Education* was an extensive reevaluation of teacher education. For that, the field owes much to Dr. Conant. While his proposals did not always delineate exactly how they were to be implemented, they were nevertheless numerous, specific and related to a larger schema, even if seemingly nonphilosophical. These factors enhanced the richness but not the depth of intellectual exchange. Conant's concreteness increased his greater favor among administrators and educationist practitioners, though not with theorists. The Faculty Senate Committee of Syracuse University asked its School of Education members to examine *The Education* and report formally on how they were or were not implementing Conant's recommendations. The School of Education Report indicated that the school was doing practically everything Conant recommended considerably before *The Education* was published. Throughout the nation, much informal evaluation has resulted. Conferences on teacher education, if not focusing directly on the report, dealt with some basic aspect of it. A Cornell University conference in April 1964 discussed the contributions of five different academic disciplines to teacher education. The first talk, on anthropology by Solon T. Kimball, began by referring to *The Education* and reiterated Kimball's view that Conant "ignores the larger issue of the function of formal education in our society." [26]

Among the most desirable results of *The Education* besides its widespread stimulation of lay interest and professional expression of ideas have been the "experiments" it has fostered both in programs of teacher education and in approaches to certification. Conant has already moved on to further endeavors in addition to his autobiography—the interstate compact and a review of his American high school study, sponsored by a $100,000 grant from the National Association of Secondary-School Principals. This most recent study, *The Comprehensive High School: A Second Report to Interested Citizens* (1967), found certain improvements but vast inequalities and shortcomings which he related to financial inequities; he therefore asked that Congress return to the states a portion of federal income tax receipts. While defining a comprehensive high school as one having both a college preparatory and a vocational track, his minimal criteria for the comprehensive high school were strictly academic: provide instruction in calculus; provide instruction in a modern language for four years; arrange scheduling so that in any one year a student may take English, mathematics, science, a foreign language, social studies, physical education and art or music; provide one or more college–level courses for able students; and have a pupil load of 120 or less for each English teacher. The 2000 high schools surveyed in this study were all of medium size; slum and suburban schools were eliminated and only a few schools in large cities were sampled.

Backed by the Carnegie Corporation and others, Conant has helped to promote a number of studies and programs currently in the developmental stage. It is too early and beyond the scope of this volume to make a detailed study of these trial innovations. Some future work will have to delineate the actual programs. Hopefully, the need for nonpartisan controlled evaluation will be recognized and implemented. This could provide empirical evidence as to the actual effectiveness of the new endeavors, in comparison to older patterns. At present, the nature of some of the tentative plans which Conant's teacher education work sparked can merely be sketched. Conant deserves considerable credit for being the major catalyst in stimulating these innovations.

In November 1964, Northwestern University, in cooperation with the Carnegie Corporation of New York, held an invitational conference entitled "Innovation in

Teacher Education." Its purpose was to bring together representatives of about twelve colleges or universities committed to the goal of improvement in teacher education "to describe institutional innovations, discuss research designs, share results of research, take advantage of consultant services (Dr. J. B. Conant has agreed to serve in that capacity), and plan further meetings." [27] At that conference, Conant clarified his "all-university approach" to mean an "all-university committee," which would have the "last say on the program," although he recognized "that this recommendation in my book is the most radical and is so radical it can be, indeed, it has been, designated as naive." [28] However, some universities, such as Oregon State, Syracuse, and Wisconsin, have had some kind of all-university pattern long before publication of *The Education*.

Conant also admitted then that, while his idea of teachers returning on a leave of absence for a semester or two to a college or university after they had completed the four-year preparation program and had started to teach "is a bit Utopian," he still felt it was "a good thing to be done." Conant stated that the least controversial of his recommendations was the one on a gradual induction period. Although he had been criticized for neglecting the "art" involved in teaching, Conant suggested that "clinical professors" might be called "professors of the teaching art." In 1966, he described as "the most radical proposal I have put forward" the recommendation "that certification should be largely up to colleges that prepare teachers rather than in the hands of the state agencies." [29]

Conant was appointed by James E. Allen Jr., then State Education Commissioner, a consultant to the New York State Department of Education on the "Five-College Project," and his project administrator, John S. Hollister, is carrying on much of that work in line with Conant's proposals. The New York department agreed to approve the departure from traditional teacher education programs by Vassar, Brooklyn College, and the State University of New York at Fredonia, Cornell, and Colgate and to certify all the graduates of those experimental programs for a five-year period. The schools were to use committees to attain an "all-university approach," develop a novel experimental design, maintain a limit of two or three academic fields for which to prepare teachers, have released time for adequate supervision of teachers, make plans to evaluate the projects, and develop budgets for a three-year implementation period.[30] Recent changes in New York State's certification requirements have provided for greater institutional autonomy.

The tentative original plans were for Vassar to stress high school social studies with a clinical professor and a materials center. Brooklyn College would focus on English and mathematics, and Fredonia on early childhood and English. Cornell was to concentrate on secondary teachers with stress on the academic-professional course distribution, new high school curricula and teaching methods, the M.A.T. program, general versus specialized preparation, practice-teaching patterns, in-service education, and the clinical professor idea. At Colgate, three tracks were to be compared: a teaching fellow program of five years granting the M.A.T. in the fifth year after four years of undergraduate work leading to the B.A. degree; a beginning teacher program involving a year of full-time teaching under supervision (and with seminars) after the B.A. degree; and an intern program for those with no professional preparation who would prepare for the M.A.T. in one or two summers and one semester of academic and professional preparation plus one semester of supervised teaching. It was hoped that such programs would be tested to gauge which might be of value to other institutions, to attract better students to teaching, and to gain more information about effective practice-teaching and the costs of these and similar programs.

At Northwestern University, a four-year curriculum was planned, which some sensational newspaper articles described as being without methods courses. However, clinical experience and tutorials were to be provided throughout the four years. The college arranged for freshmen to be tutored and to serve as tutors in the schools. As sophomores, students would continue to serve as tutors and take educational psychology for two semesters, and then decide whether to pursue a teaching career or not. As juniors, part of their time would be spent in a welfare agency, and in school studies of relationships among a board, superintendent, teachers, students, and the parent-teacher association. Their tutorial work would then concentrate on problems of learning, school organization, curriculum theory, and research design. They would attend school-board meetings, interview the board, work with the National Association of Secondary-School Principals, the guidance counselor, curriculum groups, the principal and others. Their senior clinical experience would be a student-teaching experience, part-time throughout the year, perhaps in "team teaching" under a clinical professor. In senior tutorial, students would present their rationale for teaching a subject to particular students and their ideas would be examined by both a methodology and a content professor.

Besides faculty meetings to implement the joint approach, and the enrollment of 500 to 600 quality students, the necessary contacts with the public schools, and the appointment of task forces in each subject, Northwestern University appointed five clinical assistant professors. This is one of the few cases of that recommendation being implemented. One of the questions which such experiments could help answer is whether the burden many claim the clinical person will have to carry in a Conantian program will be too great. Can one person successfully deal with theory and practice and also serve both the schools and the college or university? Realizing possible problems with this, Conant began to urge that what clinical professors needed most was recent teaching experience in those subjects and levels they were to supervise. Other difficulties to be worked out either before or during the program, which began in September 1965, were the relationship and effects of the experimental program to the traditional one, how to get sufficient preparation in all subjects (especially mathematics), whether the early saturation with the education field might drive some students out, and whether education professors would make suitable tutors.

Financed by the Carnegie Corporation, NAASP began a three-year study in some of the schools of Detroit, Richmond, and St. Louis, whereby all beginning teachers would have a reduced load in their first year and more contact with experienced teachers, who would help by observing and supervising the beginner. Local colleges were to be involved in the induction process and a half-time project coordinator would assist the novice. Five different supervisory plans were anticipated: the supervising teacher of English is relieved of two classes; the supervising teacher of English is relieved of three classes; each beginner is assigned to an experienced teacher of five different subjects; one school inducts three teachers with four classes each but few extra duties, with the supervisor also teaching four classes and being paid an extra $800 for the year; a college teacher supervises ten to fifteen social studies teachers as one-third load while the beginning teachers have a three-quarters schedule.

While the immediate controversy fomented by Conant's teacher education study has almost entirely abated, with the last major professional response appearing in January 1966, many of the outcomes of that dispute are still being determined. Experimental programs were being contemplated at Princeton and the Antioch-Putney Graduate School. In the long run, as Cremin has pointed out, the controversy itself will probably be viewed as one major skirmish among many between those of different convictions. But it may also be looked upon as the dispute which, more than any previous one, succeeded in launching experimentation in a field which has spoken for it far more frequently than it has directly implemented it in its own teacher education programs. It may also be known as the controversy that has most aided in provoking clarification of the problems and issues and in exposing the various outlooks that reflect the lack of certainty underlying the whole field. However, the phenomenal growth of the American Educational Research Association (AERA) demonstrates that Conant's success in increasing the realization of the need for further empirical research was mainly part of a technical concern and trend long preceding *The Education*.

In 1964, AACTE released its Teacher Education

and Mass Media (TEAM) Report with another teacher education model, both similar to and different from Conant's; AACTE has also sponsored a study by Harold Taylor of teacher education in relation to world affairs.[31] Internal professional and external social forces have been seeking to improve the answers to the perennial question of how the education of teachers is best accomplished. Those who maintained that improvement must come from outside the establishment seem as nearsighted in that respect as those who thought it could only come from within the establishment. The question of which will most improve the situation is presently a speculative chicken and egg one. Outside challenge is needed; so is internal professional leadership.

Despite the fact that a long-range historical perspective will reduce the enormity of a single individual's contributions, the varying orientations and issues brought to the fore by the Conant controversy deserve to periodically be reexamined and experimented with. Several, such as the theory-practice relationship, merit a much more extensive examination than could be done in this context. Such reevaluations will be especially significant if they are done without trying to prove the success of particular schemes and if more experimental programs are developed of the non-Conant as well as of the Conantian variety.

There is a need to try out Conant's academic, achievement-oriented system, with its focus on clinical aid and practice. It would also be desirable to test lengthy (e.g., two-year) graduate professional-school approaches with strong theoretical, existential, or developmental sociopsychological or aesthetic emphases, with an eye to discovering their effects on the initial and long-range teaching behavior of prospective professionals. We could thus expand our bases of comparison for judging (in terms of shared social goals) which kind of teacher education programs ought to be provided for those who choose this challenging, important, and complex occupation. Most likely, if it were administratively possible, students should have alternate programs related to their individual strengths, weaknesses, and personalities, and the nature of the teaching positions they seek. Such specialization could follow clinical experience and general liberal and professional preparation, as done in the study of medicine.

Conant's greatest contribution derives from his success in gaining the support of certain powerful organizations and officials in the posing and initiating of new teacher education and certification alternatives. We need many more. Generally, Conant's teacher education proposals have been supported by conservative and moderate social forces. But this is not to say that Conant is merely a conservative or a moderate. At the 1964 Northwestern Conference on "Innovation in Teacher Education," Conant stated:

For there is one principle I am sure of in education, from the kindergarten to the medical school, and that is that every generation you have to come up with a new set of ideas, new principles, new organizations. In the process you have to be convinced that what was done before was completely wrong, and what is being done now is completely right. And if you are convinced of that, you will be a good teacher. This is among sociologists called a Hawthorne effect. It is the most important principle in the subject we are discussing here.[32]

The education of American teachers and youth would be less a matter of concern and debate than it presently is were it not for the challenge provided by Conant. He opened Pandora's box by disclosing that neither laymen nor educators agree upon the best way of educating the teachers any more than upon the education of the pupils. How American society conducts education is inevitably linked to its ideal of a desirable adult culture. That ideal will both affect and be influenced by societal conditions and ideas, including the state of knowledge, the status of the field, and prevalent socioeducational conceptions. The degree to which emphasis will be placed in teaching on the multiplicity of elements involved, and how these are or are not to be related, will be an expression of societal conditions and aspirations. That is why each generation in an open society must redefine education.

In promoting what is generally a conventional social orientation with many innovative arrangements and procedures, Conant has made a significant contribution. More stimulating outlooks must result in specific proposals and must be administratively feasible if they are to become rooted in the practice as well as the theory of American education. This will also require a social climate receptive to such new approaches. An extensive inquiry into some of the more fundamental social and educational questions might then be evoked. As long as American society's main concern is survival, the concern with education primarily as a source of social leadership and technological talent will continue. We obviously need to consider that concern as long as it also contributes to rather than obliterates personal and individual goals.

In an interview with Conant published in March of

1967, Terry Ferrer, director of the New York editorial office of Science Research Associates, Inc. and former education editor of the now defunct *New York Herald Tribune,* quotes Conant:

I am not sure that *The Education of American Teachers* (1963) has been successful. Maybe the timing was wrong. Maybe I was not wise to delve into teacher-education reform. I was reluctant. If I had not spent the time in writing this book and in traveling around the country preaching teacher-education revision, then I would have had more time to spend on the problems of slums and their schools.[33]

Ferrer concurred with Conant's estimate of his impact since he stated that "only half-a-dozen" institutions were committed to Conant's program. But this preceded the changes in teacher certification in New York State.

To this writer, for a single volume to attain the adoption of its advocated practices in six universities is a fantastic accomplishment, but Conant sought greater influence than that. As he continues in the interview:

You don't have the political base for such a change in teacher education. Even a dozen people won't put any pressure on the vested schools of education to change their unnecessary restrictions. I'm just as dissatisfied and annoyed as I was when the teacher-education book was finished; here I'm discouraged. I still feel just as strongly about the establishment, too.[34]

Ferrer elaborated upon the last sentence by writing:

This means that he still considers the 960,000 member NEA, the regional accrediting agencies, local school boards, state departments of education, and professors of education as having neither "the interest" nor the "competence" to deal with the current problems of education. (Again, paradoxically, his latest book was written as a committee chairman of the National Association of Secondary School Principals, a division of the NEA.)[35]

In this latest interview by Ferrer, Conant continued his pleas for homogeneous ability grouping (although he acknowledged its dangers to the principle of racial equality which he now also wants honored), and for increased use of technological media such as television and programmed instruction. Never acknowledging the different viewpoints that exist, Conant again revealed his almost unquestioning faith in his educational positions as needing more to be instituted than to be evaluated by stating: "If I were twenty years younger, and had the ideas I have now, I would go up and sit in Albany as a lobbyist, and see to it that the bills to support public schools and reform teacher education got through the legislature. Political action is what's needed." [36] He is against legislative interference when it goes against something in which he believes (academic freedom) but for it when it serves his purpose (reform of teacher education). He favors the goal of institutional autonomy but advocates using legislative pressure as a way of obtaining it. He is more of an education politician than either an educational thinker or a true experimentalist.

The development of an even "greater society" than that which we presently seek mandates a concern for the individual not mainly in terms of his importance as a social "resource" affecting social welfare or the social system, but as a person in his own right. If maintaining the society or its economic or political system become the society's ends rather than its means to individual fulfillment, the society will be less democratic and less deserving of preservation. The more democratic ideal stresses educating individuals to become more independent humans, directing their own development for the realization of self and of society. Fortunately, America still retains that ideal *verbally* as a goal towards which to aim, even though we have not politically implemented it in an educational program.

Conant's goal—preserving and expanding the benefits of a free society—is especially worthy when it is remembered that the purpose of such a social goal is to realize the inherent dignity and value of every individual; to enable him to become a person who can choose his place in the widest possible social limits. Such a goal opposes a narrow subscription to any specific ideological, political, social, economic, religious, or educational dogmas or systems. It means a commitment to a constant reevaluation, preservation, or alteration of current arrangements stemming from increased involvement of self-directed, self-fulfilling "American radicals," who can consider both the values and the dangers of cooperative social economic ventures and of those resulting from independent private enterprise, and from mixed economies. Human development and economic profit have too long been seen as mutually exclusive values. They need not be opposed to each other; but our society mostly preaches the former while practicing the latter. The "Great Society" needs to be defined in terms of its ability to foster and value great persons rather than assassinate them.

It should be no surprise that less conservative "American radicals" trying to revise practice in terms of humanistic (not merely functional or realistic) ideals, should be seen by Conant as naive optimists who do not realize that the school cannot directly change the society it must reflect. In a free society, schools must foster the reevaluation of the basic social patterns, not merely uncritically transmit them as is done in totalitarian societies. We cannot ignore the fact that the struggle to accomplish a reevaluation will often run counter to the concerns of enlightened societal leaders, who may correctly fear a possible loss of power. But merely to follow a status quo socialization induction process (whether subject matter or pupil or societal centered) and to call it education, is to undermine the very foundation of a free society. To psychologize education from a social viewpoint need not deintellectualize it. We need lifeadjustment in its fullest aesthetic, intellectual, personal, physical, practical, and social sense; not merely a lifeaccommodation whether promulgated by academicians or educationists.

Although we now accept competition within a cooperative framework, the pressures of a technological society will continue to emphasize the corporate system rather than the individual. Authority and discipline will need to be balanced with a stress on freedom, prescription with election, and objective matters with realization of the subjective so as to produce evaluation and not merely measurement. Adjustment will need to be seen as a two-way interactive process, not merely accommodation. Standards will need to incorporate both academic and personal-social variables, and be blended with acceptance. A continuing university hierarchy will increasingly emphasize subject matter more than the student, social ends more than self-fulfillment, and "efficient," "professional" arrangements and impersonal technology more than personal situations. Cognitive factors are likely to be stressed rather than affective and aesthetic ones; and striving, social mobility, and achievement will be given more weight than choice of patterns, including affiliation and social stability. Administratively easy, inexpensive organization will continue to be the practice rather than the design of desirable patterns for human learning. Specialized depth will, in effect, be stressed over exploratory breadth. The science of teaching will be emphasized more than the art. Organized knowledge will continue to receive more attention than consequential personal-social and societal problems and issues. If students continue to react and grow as a constructive rather than destructive power factor in higher education, we may obtain the needed balanced blend of all these values.

The capacity and ability of the learner will be taken into account more than his interests and motivation. If ability is perceived as fixed more by heredity than by environment, and attempts are not increased and improved to equalize the latter, we will face the dangers of revolutionary rather than evolutionary change. We already speak of overachievers as well as underachievers, but I am not sure how any person can overachieve. Increased need for mental skills should lead us to expect more homogeneous ability-tracking over heterogeneous grouping and more Jeffersonianism than Jacksonianism. The greater emphasis on mental skills will, hopefully, be part of the developmental, emotional, psychological, social, and moral aspects of life. As higher education becomes increasingly important, concern with the talented is also likely to grow at a faster rate than concern with the average and slow learner.

Technology could lead to product being stressed more than process, but means more than ends. Science will continue to reign over philosophy, humanities, arts, and social studies (except as applied), and the latter areas will gain recognition by asserting themselves as increasingly scientifically objective. A recent article in *The New York Times Magazine* (January 28, 1968) stressed the "structuralism" of French ethnologist Claude Levi-Straus, who debates frequently with existentialist Jean-Paul Sarte. While Conant speaks for very cautiously applying empiricism to human matters, and Dewey wanted scientific method (in its larger sense) applied to human affairs, the *Times* article explains that Levi-Straus approaches the social sciences as he does the natural and physical ones:

"Structuralism," says Levi-Straus, "is the search for unsuspected harmonies. It is the discovery of a system of relations latent in a series of objects."

It is based on the idea that human behavior can be classified scientifically like a plant or a chemical element. Why should there be anything arbitrary in man? There must be laws governing human behavior just as there are laws governing pollenization or cellular growth. Levi-Straus believes you can study a tribe the same way a biologist studies an amoeba.[37]

Increasing awareness of the transitory and tenuous nature of a fast-changing life is causing us to learn to live with uncertainty, not by facing it, as Dewey once asked, but by either cautiously postulating an objectivism, as Conant does, or by fully accepting it, in the manner of Levi-Straus. Idealists would hold that the investigator creatively produces his relations; realists, that he discovers them; and pragmatists, that it comes from the interaction of both an individual's conceptions and his verified or corroborated perceptions. Today's reas-

sertion of realism has already meant stressing facts over
values, concrete matters over abstract thought, objective
aspects over subjective ones, empirical data over rationalist theory, the inductive measurable over deductive
examination of scientific models, and descriptive reality
over normative considerations. Both Dewey and Conant have granted the two modes, but Conant once
again not only sees these as too distinct but also
expresses a strong, subjective preference for the realist
side in educational matters.

We certainly need to be concerned with the application of science, not merely technology, to education.
Yet, this ought to encompass realization of its normative as well as its descriptive aspects. To neglect the subjective quicksand on which we may be building our
objectivity can, as uncomfortable as that may be, serve
only to decrease that objectivity. Idealism as well as materialism are part of reality and though distinct, they are
not as separate and unrelated as some realists conceive.
Such a Godlike notion of scientific objectivity may
actually help to perpetuate pedagogical fads and extremes in socioeducational philosophy as humans respond and react to changes in societal conditions as
though they were each time perceiving "Truth." Even
great literature may soon be evaluated by computerized
techniques. Emotions and feelings might be relegated
to education's wastebasket as unworthy of consideration
in contrast to the demonstrable proofs of mathematical
linguistic symbols. In fact, such symbols are presently in
the frontier of educational research.

Both individual and societal needs will have to be
assessed if we are to attain society's commitment to educating for the overall growth and development of each
and every individual in relation to the kind of person he

or she chooses to become. No person or system can ever accomplish such a utopian goal; but neither can they claim to be promoting a liberal education for a free society if there is no commitment to increasing the number of educators seeking to work towards that goal. Conant's contribution is mainly, but not exclusively, to the national side of the ledger; Taylor's is primarily, but not exclusively, to the personal-social side. Social forces now support the Conant emphasis. Both aspects are needed if a fully liberal education is to result. The existentialist viewpoint is important not as a philosophy for education but as a challenge to the attainment of a better balance for both society and the individual. To neglect the future as existentialists do, is short-sighted; to ignore the here and now in which we live, as some overly achievement-oriented educators do, is far-sighted. Balanced vision is needed. Lack of adjustment of the established educational institutions to the emerging social forces will lead either to more urban education crises or to new institutions such as the storefront schools.

Today, more social scientists, educators, and even psychologists are being employed to help manage and maintain the system, and to prevent a dissatisfied class or group from overthrowing it. Enlightened leaders will also have to exert their skills not only to keep sight of the individual in this process but also to help develop in our cities the most humane orientation a technocracy can afford. The riots are as much a social-class protest as they are racial. Conant has attempted this humane orientation, with his longstanding preference for liberal education, but it is too traditionally defined. Enlightened educators will have to borrow and develop new and more effective techniques to compete with the commercial and presently dominant political forces.

These forces will resist voluntary cooperative economic arrangements which threaten, rather than enhance, the position of the entrenched governmental, industrial, professional, and labor-managerial classes.

Like other citizens, most educators are not personally or as a group free enough of these powerful influences to refrain unconsciously or consciously, from serving their purposes. It will take commitment, competence, and courage to delineate preventive rather than merely remedial approaches to the problems of white superiority, school dropouts or pushouts, lack of concern and understanding of international realities and possibilities, and middle and lower class urban crime and violence, to say nothing of mental health, high anxiety, and the unemployable unskilled.

Conant is not alone in wanting to keep the social system, including present educational agencies, going in order to attain the ideal of societal improvement. Focusing on both rational and social-personal factors can provide the means and conditions for individual fulfillment. This is the basic goal, whether specified in Conant's or Taylor's or my terms, or chosen (as it inevitably must be) by each individual for himself. Individual fulfillment needs to be more widely viewed in its necessary social context.

School personnel must somehow learn to allow for pluralistic options without prejudicial treatment. Then Taylor's and Conant's proposals, or my combination or other alternatives, would be real choices. Schools and school systems would not have to be structured according to one philosophy, metaphysical or not. Teachers and students could be freer to be themselves in a system where acceptance of the standards of each would, where possible, determine the course of courses of action. In such a system, students would have a determining role along with teachers and teacher educators. Such an orientation would foster a variety of possibilities in different schools, in the same school, and even in the same class. Neither the present system nor the Conantian approach that fits it could remain the same. There would be room for much more variety and pluralism, perhaps even honest exploration in public schools among competing philosophical and religious options as well as social-political and economic alternatives. Public schools also need more of the institutional autonomy that Conant has opposed for them, but which he seeks for higher education and approved teacher education institutions.

Freedom will only be preserved if we do not merely conserve our society with its values and goods, but also promote a more humanistic society stressing social criticism and higher ideals. We can not accomplish this merely by inducting youth into personal success patterns in the present culture. There will have to be revision of the traditional academic cultural induction pattern, as well as of the model-type induction approaches to teacher education. The first is especially needed because the increasing numbers of people, including prospective teachers, have vastly more academic than professional studies. More cooperative, democratic approaches among teachers, parents, administrators, and students will be needed to replace the authoritarian school structures that attract and reward "system" teachers at all educational levels.

The problem is not merely that of attaining real cooperation between academicians and professionals but of developing a societal climate that values true cooperation among those of different persuasions who are sincerely trying to use various kinds of knowledge to solve our social and educational problems. The conflict between academicians and educationists merely reflects the status seeking of individuals in a mechanized impersonal society in a high state of flux. Either Utopian idealists or overly extreme realists can impede progress. While seeking to improve and extend our advanced civilization, we must continually reassess our social and educational goals and decide how we can actually move closer to them.

The dominant established system and the extreme yet badly needed reactions like existentialism, Summerhill and Summerlane could be replaced by the kind of balance Professor Paul Nash of Boston University sought in his *Freedom and Authority in Education* (1966): the authority to work with the freedom to play; the authority of institutions with the freedom to think, teach, and learn; the authority of discipline with the freedom to develop one's own interests; the authority of the group with the freedom to become oneself; the authority of excellence with the freedom to choose; the authority of tradition with the freedom to create; and the authority of commitment with the freedom to grow.[38] Traditionalists like Conant tend to stress the authority side of the ledger. Progressives and existentialists emphasize the freedom aspects. More libertarian protests are now needed to force a true dialogue out of which might come a synthesis which could enhance human development on societal, interpersonal, and individual bases.

Some thinkers of diverse political persuasions are protesting the present system. Students are asking for a voice in the decisions affecting their educational lives. Humanity waves, although distrusted by Conant, still

seem the only answer to the Hegelianlike currents he
also opposes. When basic human concerns are no
longer relegated to a subordinate place in the curriculum of American education, and when educators themselves face both the individual and societal nature of
their roles, it may then be possible to decrease progressive thrusts and conservative reactions in education as
in society.

It remains the basic task of American educators (academic and professional) to provide the enlightened
leadership and knowledge popular thrusts deserve and
need. In contrast to communist or fascist cultures, the
concerns of all the people will be served, rather than
those of an elite economic, political, religious, social, or
educational group. In order to prevent the latter alternative, teacher educators will themselves have to be in
closer contact with the aspirations of the deprived
classes to understand that they are not so different from
their own needs and efforts. The teachers then will be
more accessible to the children and teacher-educators to
the teachers, instead of being merely a new aristocratic
"meritocracy" concerned primarily with perpetuating
and strengthening its own professional and social position. At one college, the education division opposed
expanding a Project Opportunity for lower-class students and of adding a New York State "Search for Education, Elevation, and Knowledge" (SEEK) program
until there was more data on the initial thirty students
of a student body of 4,000. As one conservative professor said, "Who wants all those black-power and S.D.S.
(Students for a Democratic Society) types around?"
Resistance to certain socioeducational changes is to be
expected, but the changes are in the making.

A humane outlook is essential to American society

and education. Democracy's best long range interests and defense lie in the defining and implementing of its own societal, social, interpersonal, and individual ideals. Educators can help to fulfill that need by trying to combine the concerns of hard-nosed realists like James Bryant Conant with those of idealist romanticists like Paul Goodman and Harold Taylor rather than merely having each group attacking the other.[39] We must be able to develop and change concrete organizational structures so that administration becomes a humanized means of fostering the attainment of the reinforcing educational aims of personal and intellectual development and societal advancement. Until college officials invent and adopt a feasible substitute for the academic credit and marking system, such as the free university system where students select their professors and curriculum, there are still other specific changes which might be contemplated. For example, abolishing the outmoded hierarchical clerical and military model of academic rank and titles in higher education could lead to more open and honest competition and cooperation in regard to different conceptions of the good life and of what these imply for education at all levels, especially for those who attain the highest privilege and responsibility—that of being teachers of children.

Greater power for parents and students, which has both constructive and destructive possibilities, is now a fact that administrators and teachers must confront, although Conant avoids dealing with these realities as they bear on teacher education. The new forces should help establish the meaning of professionalism in education as real service to the clients—the children and their parents and, in teacher education, the prospective, non fully-certified and inservice teachers. No longer will professionalism be primarily, or merely, a matter of job protection for the established members of the teaching business.

Education and schooling will not be synonymous then, as Conant tends to treat them despite his awareness in some writings but denials in others that the two are not even necessarily acknowledged the same in practice. Depending on how education as an activity is defined (Conant avoids giving such a definition), it is possible, as Conant granted in reference to Nazi Germany, that education and schooling could be mutually exclusive terms.

In teacher education, we need to help prospective and practicing teachers develop certain conceptions of education lacked by Conant so that they will educate, not indoctrinate or merely train and induct their students. This demands both an intellectually rational educational philosophy and an explicitly delineated personal sociopsychological approach, which Conant lacks.

To present a personal orientation as being based on results objectively derived from unbiased, unselected, raw data, and to hide this philosophy behind a pseudo-scientific empirical cloak is a highly questionable professional practice, especially in education and particularly where the facts are not the results of controlled experimentation, or real scientific empiricism. Put simply, Conant's facts merely supported his prejudices. Whether his biases are adequate to our individual and society's cultural needs as we move into the seventies is the question probed in this book. My answer is that without the kind of expansion and modification previously suggested, they definitely are not adequate to the present or emerging needs of our society. Each reader will, of course, have to draw his or her own conclusions.

Notes

1. E. O. Melby, *American Education under Fire: The Story of the "Phony Three-R Fight"* (New York: Anti-Defamation League of B'nai B'rith, 1951); and W. W. Brickman, "Attack and Counterattack in American Education," *School and Society*, LXXIV (October 27, 1951), 262–269.

2. For a description and analysis of some of the questionable attacks on American education in the 1950's, see *Progressive Education*, XXIX (January 1952). The entire issue is devoted to "Meeting the Attacks on Education." The pamphlet "How Red is the Little Red School House?" is mentioned on p. 73 as being published by the Employers Association of Chicago.

3. "Schools Make News," *Saturday Review*, January 21, 1967, p. 73.

4. M. I. Berger, "Existential Criticism in Educational Theory: A Subjective View of a Serious Business," *Proceedings of the Nineteenth Annual Meeting of the Philosophy of Education Society* (Lawrence: University of Kansas Press, 1963), p. 96.

5. Koerner's case-building can be seen by comparing the full data and text of Robert M. Weiss and Glen R. Rasmussen, "Grading Practices in Undergraduate Education Courses," *The Journal of Higher Education*, XXXI (March 1960), 143–149, with Koerner, *The Miseducation of American Teachers* (Boston: Houghton Mifflin, 1963), p. 137.

6. Two outstanding anthologies of attacks and criticisms of public education are: Ernest O. Melby and Morton Puner, eds., *Freedom and Public Education* (New York: Praeger, 1953) and C. Winfield Scott and Clyde M. Hill, eds., *Public Education Under Criticism* (Englewood Cliffs, N.J.: Prentice Hall, 1954).

7. James B. Conant, "The Superintendent Was the Target," *The New York Times Book Review*, April 29, 1951, pp. 1, 27, a review of David Hulburd's *This Happened in Pasadena* (New York: Macmillan, 1951); and "Education: Engine of Democracy" in "The Private School Controversy," *Saturday Review*, May 3, 1952, p. 12.

8. Earle U. Rugg, "Who Shall Be Educated for Teaching?" *Journal of Teacher Education*, XVI (June 1965), 223.

9. James B. Conant, *The Child, the Parent, and the State* (New York: McGraw-Hill, 1965), pp. 1–2.

10. James B. Conant, stenotyped manuscript of Conference on Teacher Education, Northwestern University, November 16–17, 1964, p. 209.

11. *Philosophy in the Education of Teachers*, joint report of the Committee on Philosophy in Education of the American Philosophical Association, and the Committee on Cooperation with the American Philosophical Association of the Philosophy of Education Society, p. 5, reprinted from *Proceedings and Addresses of the American Philosophical Association, 1958–1959*, XXXII (October 1959). See also Joe R. Burnett, "Conant on the Philosophy of Education," *Educational Theory*, XIV (January 1964), 24–30.

12. Solon T. Kimball and James E. McClellan, *Education and the New America* (New York: Random House, 1962), p. 24.

13. Paul Goodman, *Compulsory Mis-Education and The Community of Scholars* (New York: Random House, 1966), pp. 217–218.

14. James B. Conant, *Education and Liberty: The Role of the Schools in a Modern Democracy* (Cambridge, Mass.: Harvard University Press, 1953), p. 87.

15. James B. Conant, "The Future of Our Higher Education," *Harpers Magazine*, May 1938, p. 570.

16. Lawrence A. Cremin, *The Genius of American Education* (New York: Random House, 1966), pp. 92–93.

17. See Leonard Kenneth Kise, *A Comparison of Some Effects Upon Teacher Candidates of Two Kinds of Professional Education Preparatory Programs.* Unpublished Ph.D. dissertation, Cornell University, 1964.

18. For examples, see Joe R. Burnett, "Some Observations on the Logical Implications of Philosophic Theory for Educational Theory and Practice," *Proceedings of the Fourteenth Annual Meeting of the Philosophy of Education Society* (Lawrence: University of Kansas Press, 1958), pp. 51–57; and Hobert Burns, "The Logic of the 'Educational Implication,'" *Proceedings of the Sixteenth Annual Meeting of the Philosophy of Education Society* (Lawrence: University of Kansas Press, 1960), pp. 49–55.

19. George L. Newsome, Jr., "In What Sense Is Theory a Guide to Practice in Education?" *Educationary Theory*, XIV (January 1964), 39.

20. James B. Conant, *Shaping Educational Policy* (New York: McGraw-Hill, 1964), p. 82.

21. Myron S. Lieberman, *Education as a Profession* (Englewood Cliffs, N.J.: Prentice-Hall, 1956), pp. 157–184.

22. A. E. Joyal, "The National Council for Accreditation of Teacher Education in 1963," *Report on the NCATE Conference of One Hundred* (Washington, D.C.: American Association of Colleges for Teacher Education, 1964), p. 5.

23. James B. Conant, "On Taking Education Seriously," *The Reporter*, December 3, 1964, p. 19.

24. "Wisconsin *v.* NCATE," *School and Society*, LXXXXI

(Summer 1963), 236. See also Lindley J. Stiles, "Reorganizing Accreditation for Teacher Education," *Phi Delta Kappan*, XLV (October 1963), 31–37; and for a contrasting view, Chester C. Travelstead, "NCATE Yesterday, Today, and Tomorrow," *Phi Delta Kappan* XLV (October 1963), 38–41.

25. John R. Mayor, *Accreditation in Teacher Education: Its Influence on Higher Education* (Washington, D.C.: The National Commission on Accrediting, 1965), p. 231.

26. Solon T. Kimball, "Anthropology and Teacher Education," in D. B. Gowen and Cynthia Richardson, eds., *Five Fields and Teacher Education* (Cornell University: Project One Publications, 1965), p. 1.

27. *Innovation in Teacher Education*, report of a conference at Northwestern University, November 16–17, 1964 in cooperation with the Carnegie Corporation of New York (Evanston, Ill.: Northwestern University Press, 1965), p. 4.

28. Conant, stenotyped Conference on Teacher Education, *op. cit.*, p. 12.

29. "Dr. James B. Conant Answers Questions You Ask About Schools," *Changing Times*, XX January 1966, 27.

30. The information about these and other programs are primarily from notes given to me by John S. Hollister. Hollister used the notes to prepare the talk on "Recent Experimentation and Innovation in Teacher Education" he gave at Penn State in April 1965.

31. Herbert F. LaGrone, *A Proposal for the Revision of the Pre-Service Professional Component of a Program of Teacher Education: A Project to Improve the Professional Sequence in Pre-Service Teacher Education Through the Selective and Planned Use of New Media* (Washington, D.C.: AACTE, 1964); and Harold Taylor, "The Teacher in the World," *Humanist*, January–February, 1968, pp. 16–19.

32. Conant, stenotyped Conference on Teacher Education, *op. cit.*, pp. 207–208.
33. Terry Ferrer, "Conant Revisited," *Saturday Review*, March 18, 1967, pp. 57, 73.
34. *Ibid.*, p. 73.
35. *Ibid.*
36. *Ibid.*
37. Sanche de Gramont, "There Are No Superior Societies," *The New York Times Magazine*, January 28, 1968, p. 28.
38. Paul Nash, *Authority and Freedom in Education: An Introduction to the Philosophy of Education* (New York: Wiley, 1966).
39. For sympathetic analyses of the movement in education from idealism to realism, see Peter Schrag's "Teachers College: John Dewey with a Hard Nose," *Saturday Review*, December 16, 1967, pp. 62–64, 75–76, and his "Education's 'Romantic' Critics," *Saturday Review*, February 18, 1967, pp. 80–82, 98–99.

Bibliography*

I. REFERENCES ON TEACHER EDUCATION

American Council on Education. *The Improvement of Teacher Education: A Final Report by the Commission on Teacher Education*. Washington, D.C.: American Council on Education, 1946.

Armstrong, W. Earl. *The Education of Teachers: Retrospect and Prospect*. Kirksville, Mo.: Simpson Printing Co., 1964.

Borrowman, Merle. *The Liberal and Technical in Teacher Education: A Historical Survey of American Thought*. New York: Bureau of Publications, Teachers College, Columbia University, 1956.

Brubacher, John S., and Willis Rudy. *Higher Education in Transition: An American History, 1636–1956*. New York: Harper & Row, 1958.

Butts, R. Freeman. *The College Charts Its Course: Historical Conceptions and Current Proposals*. New York: McGraw-Hill, 1939.

The College Supervisor: Conflict and Challenge. Forty-third yearbook. The Association for Student Teaching. Dubuque, Iowa: William C. Brown, 1964.

Elsbree, Willard J. *The American Teacher: Evolution of*

---

* Works previously cited in the text and notes of this volume are not repeated in the Bibliography because of space considerations.

a Profession in a Democracy. New York: American Book, 1939.

Harper, Charles A. *A Century of Public Teacher Education: The Story of the State Teachers Colleges as They Evolved from the Normal Schools.* Washington, D.C.: American Association of Teachers Colleges, 1939.

Hodenfield, G. K., and T. M. Stinnett. *The Education of Teachers: Conflict and Consensus.* Englewood Cliffs, N.J.: Prentice-Hall, 1961.

Huggett, A. J., and T. M. Stinnett. *Professional Problems of Teachers,* 2d ed. New York: Macmillan, 1963.

Kinney, Lucien B. *Certification in Education.* Englewood Cliffs, N.J.: Prentice-Hall, 1964.

Lindsay, Margaret, ed. *New Horizons for the Teaching Profession.* Washington, D.C.: National Education Association, 1961.

Monroe, Walter S. *Teacher-Learning Theory and Teacher Education, 1890 to 1950.* Urbana: University of Illinois Press, 1952.

National Commission on Teacher Education and Professional Standards. *Milestones in Teacher Education and Professional Standards.* Washington, D.C.: National Education Association, 1964.

Pangburn, Jessie M. *The Evolution of the American Teachers College.* New York: Bureau of Publications, Teachers College, Columbia University, 1932.

Rudolph, Frederick. *The American College and University: A History.* New York: Knopf, 1962.

Sarason, Seymour B., Kenneth Davidson, and Burton Blatt. *The Preparation of Teachers: An Unstudied Problem in Education.* New York: Wiley, 1962.

Smith, Elmer, ed. *Teacher Education: A Reappraisal.* New York: Harper & Row, 1962.

United States Office of Education. *National Survey of the Education of Teachers.* Washington, D.C.: Government Printing Office, Bulletin 1933, Vol. VI, No. 10.

Wiggins, Sam P. *Battlefields in Teacher Education*. Nashville, Tenn.: George Peabody College for Teachers, 1964.

Woodring, Paul. *New Directions in Teacher Education*. New York: The Fund for the Advancement of Education, 1957.

II. WORKS BY JAMES B. CONANT

The only previously published Conant bibliography is by one of his secretaries: Virginia Proctor. "Bibliography of James B. Conant," *Journal of General Education*, Vol. V (October 1950), pp. 48–56. Because of space limitations, works in that bibliography are not repeated below. With the exception of Conant's technical scientific writings (most of which were articles in the *Journal of American Chemical Society* and the *Journal of Biological Chemistry*), an almost complete Conant bibliography can be constructed by combining the works in the Proctor bibliography with those cited in the text and notes of this volume and those listed below.

"Academic Independence," *American Association of University Professors Bulletin*, Vol. XXXVIII (December 1952), pp. 517–519.

"American High School." *North Central Association Quarterly*, Vol. XXXIII (April 1959), pp. 270–272.

The American High School Today. New York: McGraw-Hill, 1959.

"Athletics: The Poison Ivy in Our Schools." *Look*, January 17, 1961, pp. 56–60.

"Challenge Facing Our High School." *Wisconsin Journal of Education*, Vol. XCI (November 1958), pp. 5–8.

"Citadel of Learning." *Yale Review*, Vol. XLV (September 1955), pp. 48–61.

"Conant Looks at the Junior High School." *The Nation's*

Schools, Vol. LXV (April 1960), pp. 82, 118, 120, 124.

"Conant on the Gifted Child and the High School Curriculum." *Phi Delta Kappan*, Vol. XXXIX (April 1958), p. 340.

Creativity of Gifted and Talented Children. New York: Bureau of Publications, Teachers College, Columbia University, 1959.

"Development of Talent in Europe and the United States." *North Central Association Quarterly*, Vol. XXXIV (April 1960), pp. 265–272.

"Digest of Twenty-One Recommendations for High Schools." *Catholic Schools Journal*, Vol. LIX (September 1959), p. 72.

"Diversified Studies for Diversified Students." *National Parent-Teacher*, Vol. LIII (October 1958), pp. 4–6.

"Dr. Conant's 18 Points on Junior High Schools." *California Journal of Secondary Education*, Vol. XXXV (November 1960), pp. 443–451.

"Education and Liberty: A Look Ahead." *Virginia Quarterly Review*, Vol. XXVIII (October 1952), pp. 500–517.

"Education for Freedom." *Baltimore Bulletin of Education*, Vol. XXVII (June 1950), pp. 1–8.

"Education in the Western World." *Atlantic Monthly*, Vol. CC (November 1957), pp. 73–77.

"Education of the Academically Talented in Europe and the United States." *Middle States Association of College and Secondary Schools Proceedings* (1958), pp. 41–70.

"False Education for Many Slum Children?" *Ladies Home Journal*, January 1962, p. 6.

The Federal Republic of Germany, Our New Ally: A Lecture by James B. Conant, Former Ambassador to the Federal Republic of Germany, Delivered at the University of Minnesota Williams Arena on February 24, 1957. Minneapolis: University of Minnesota, 1957.

"Freedom and the University." *National Education Asso-*

ciation Journal, Vol. XXXIX (November 1950), pp. 581–582.

"Gifted Ones." *Newsweek*, January 23, 1956, p. 95.

"Goals of the University in the Free World." *U.S. Department of State Bulletin*, Vol. XXXIII (November 21, 1955), pp. 837–842.

"Harvard, Present and Future." *School and Society*, Vol. XLIII (April 4, 1936), pp. 449–456.

"Has the European System of Education Anything For Us?" *Parents' Magazine*, Vol. XXXIV (November 1959), p. 60.

"How to Improve Our High Schools." *National School Boards Association, Improving Education: A Free People's Responsibility*. San Jose, Calif.: Moore & Minor, 1959, pp. 171–179.

"Individual Development and the National Need: A False Antithesis." *Bulletin of the National Association of Secondary School Principals*, Vol. XLIV (April 1960), pp. 383–394.

"An Introductory Statement" and "Conference Summary." *The Identification and Education of the Academically Talented Student in the American Secondary School*. Washington, D.C.: National Education Association, 1958, pp. 15–17, 135–140.

Invitational Conference on the Academically Talented Secondary School Pupil. Washington, D.C.: National Education Association, 1958.

"Invitational Conference on the Academically Talented Secondary School Pupil." *California Journal of Secondary Education*, Vol. XXXIV (June 1959), p. 537.

"The Junior High School Years." *Saturday Review*, October 15, 1960, pp. 81–83.

"A National Philosophy," in A. Graig Baird, ed. *Representative American Speeches: 1948–1949*. New York: H. W. Wilson, Co., 1949, pp. 165–173.

"New Conant Report: Excerpts." *Senior Scholastic*, Vol. LXXIX (October 18, 1961), pp. 17–37.

"Open Letter to America's Grand-Children." *Virginia Journal of Education*, Vol. XXXVI (November 1959), p. 8.

"Our Children's Crucial Age." *Look*, April 12, 1960, p. 41.

"Our Common Heritage." *Institute of International Education News Bulletin*, Vol. XXVII (May 1952), p. 3–6.

Our Future in the Atomic Age. New York: Foreign Policy Association, 1951.

"Our High Schools Can Be Better." *Illinois Education*, Vol. XLVII (September 1958), pp. 11–14.

"Our Schools Are What We Make Them." *Ladies Home Journal*, April 1950, pp. 11, 258.

"Plastic Ball." *Time*, September 17, 1951, p. 57.

"Prestige Image and Industrial Education." *Industrial Arts and Vocational Education*, Vol. L (January 1961), p. 15.

"Public Concern for All American Youth." *Ladies Home Journal*, May 1960, p. 30.

"Public High School and the National Interest," *Bulletin of the National Association of Secondary School Principals*, Vol. XXXXII (April 1958), pp. 343–356.

Recommendations for Education in the Junior High School: a Memorandum to School Boards. Princeton, N.J.: Educational Testing Service, 1960.

"Recommendations for Education in the Junior High School Years." *National Education Association Journal*, Vol. XLIX (November 1960), pp. 18–19.

"Role of Education After the High School in Moving Freedom Forward." *National Education Association Proceedings*, Vol. XCV (1957), pp. 105–108.

Rothney, John W. M., and Bert A. Roens. *Guidance of American Youth*, "Foreword." Cambridge, Mass.: Harvard University Press, 1959.

"Scholarly Inquiry and the American Tradition." *The Educational Record*, Vol. XXXI (July 1950), pp. 275–282.

"Selective Principles in American Colleges," in Erich A.

Walter, ed. *Essay Annual.* Chicago: Scott, Foresman & Co., 1937, pp. 203–215.

"Skeptical Chemist Looks Into a Crystal Ball." *Representative American Speeches* (1951), pp. 137–147.

"Slums and Suburbs." With W. D. Boutwell. *P.T.A. Magazine,* Vol. LVI (February 1962), p. 11.

"Social Dynamite in Our Large Cities." *Vital Speeches of the Day,* Vol. XXVII (July 1, 1961), pp. 554–560.

"Some Problems of American High Schools." *Child Study,* Vol. XXXV (Fall 1958), pp. 26–32.

"Some Problems in Junior High Schools." *Bulletin of the National Association of Secondary School Principals,* Vol. XXXXIV (April 1960), pp. 310–322.

"Some Problems of the American High School: A Preliminary Report of the Conant Study," *Phi Delta Kappan,* Vol. XL (November 1, 1958), pp. 50–55.

"Superintendent as Educational Statesman," in American Association of School Administrators, *Your AASA in 1957–58.* Washington, D.C.: American Association of School Administrators, 1958, pp. 170–183.

"Two Year College for ALL?" *Newsweek,* September 22, 1952, p. 73.

"Unique Characteristics of American Public Education." *National Education Association Proceedings,* Vol. XCVI (1958), pp. 77–85.

"Unique Features of Our American Schools." *Bulletin of the National Association of Secondary School Principals,* Vol. XL (May 1956), pp. 5–14.

"What is Science?" *Bulletin of the National Association of Secondary School Principals,* Vol. XXXIV (April 1950), pp. 166–168.

III. WORKS ABOUT JAMES B. CONANT AND *The Education*

Anderson, Archbald W., Joe R. Burnett, and Frank Klassen, eds. "Discussion Report on *The Education of American Teachers.*" *Educational Theory,* Vol. XV (October 1965), pp. 333–340.

Anderson, W., D. E. Griffiths, J. C. Payne, Florence Beaman, and M. R. Fields. *Reactions to the Book by James B. Conant.* New York: New York University School of Education, 1963 (mimeo).

Brown, John Mason. "Two College Presidents." *Saturday Review of Literature,* January 8, 1949, pp. 30–32.

Bush, Robert N. "Dr. Conant and the Education of Teachers." *Journal of Secondary Education,* Vol. XXXVI (April 1961), pp. 193–196.

Cartwright, William H. "Improving the Preparation of Teachers." *Educational Forum,* Vol. XXVIII (January 1964), pp. 187–197.

Chandler, B. J. "The Conant Report and Illinois," *Chicago Sunday Sun-Times,* October 13, 1963, Section 2, pp. 1–3.

Chase, F. S. "Does the Conant Plan Actually Go Far Enough? *Chicago Sunday Sun-Times,* October 13, 1963, Section 2, p. 3.

Chase, Francis S. "On The Education of American Teachers." *Freedom With Responsibility in Teacher Education: Seventeenth Yearbook-1964 Annual Meeting.* Washington, D.C.: The American Association of Colleges for Teacher Education, 1964, pp. 36–42.

"Columbia Teachers College President Fischer and Wisconsin University Education School Dean Stiles, Give Reactions to Dr. Conant's Book." *The New York Times,* October 20, 1963, Section IV, p. 9.

"Conant Follow-up: Effects of Publication of *Education of*

American Teachers." Senior Scholastic, Vol. LXXXIII (December 6, 1963), p. 1.

"The Conant Opinionaire." *Freedom With Responsibility in Teacher Education: Seventeenth Yearbook 1964 Annual Meeting*. Washington, D.C.: The American Association of Colleges for Teacher Education, 1964, pp. 43–49.

"Conant to Survey Teacher Education." *School and Society*, Vol. LXXXIX (April 22, 1961), p. 196.

"Conant vs. The Establishment." *Time*, February 28, 1964. p. 64.

Cowley, W. H. "Conant and Dodds." *Journal of Higher Education*, Vol. IV (December 1933), pp. 455–460.

"Dr. Conant on Teacher Training, Urges on-the-job Training of Teachers." *The New York Times*, January 10. 1963, p. 7.

"Dr. Conant Plans Two-Year Study of Teacher Education under Carnegie Corporation Grant." *The New York Times*, February 6, 1961, p. 11.

"Dr. Conant's Recommendations on Teacher Education and Excerpts from Concluding Observations." *The New York Times*, September 15, 1963, p. 82.

"Dr. Conant to Publish a Book, The Education of American Teachers," *The New York Times*, August 8, 1963, p. 25.

Douglass, Paul F. "Conant's Concepts of University Administration." *Journal of Higher Education*, Vol. XXV (February 1954), pp. 59–64.

Douglass, Paul F. "Conant's Intellectual Virus." *Harvard Educational Review*, Vol. XXIV (Winter 1954), pp. 1–5.

"The Education of American Teachers." *NEA Journal*, Vol. LIII (April 1964), pp. 49–53.

"F. M. Hechinger Discusses Areas of Accord and Conflict Between Dr. Conant and Commission on Teacher Education and Professional Standards." *The New York Times*, November 24, 1963, Section IV, p. 7.

Fries, A. C. "Dr. Conant on Teacher Education." *The Balance Sheet*, Vol. XLV (January 1964), p. 195.

Greene, Maxine. "Conant and the Perilous Profession: A Review Essay." *The Journal of Higher Education*, Vol. XXXV (February 1964), pp. 104–109.

Hechinger, Fred M. "Dr. Conant's Bombshell." *The Reporter*, September 26, 1963, pp. 44–46.

Laycock, Frank. "Division and Dialogue in the House of Learning." *Saturday Review*, Vol. XLVII, September 19, 1964, pp. 58–61 and 75.

"Professor O. B. Goodman Disputes Denn, Urges Careful Study of Conant Proposals." *The New York Times*, October 2, 1963, p. 40.

"Profile." *Saturday Review*, Vol. XLIII, No. 42 (October 15, 1960), 88–89.

"A Quarrel Among Educators." *Saturday Review*, September 21, 1963, pp. 53–55, 73–74.

Robinson, Don L. "Comes the Revolution in Teacher Education. *Phi Delta Kappan*, Vol. XLV (June 1964), p. 425.

Seckinger, Richard K. "Conant on Education as a Discipline." *History of Education Quarterly*, Vol. IV (September 1964), pp. 193–197.

"Some Proposals to Improve Teacher Education Drawn from the Book, *The Education of American Teachers*." *The New York Times*, September 15, 1963, p. 1.

"Teaching of Teachers: A National Scandal?" *U.S. News and World Report*, September 30, 1963, p. 10.

Van Patten, James. "A Search for Substance in Conant's Educational Writings." *The Journal of Teacher Education*, Vol. XVI (June 1965), pp. 193–201.

Woodring, Paul. "Conant's Report on Teacher Education." *Saturday Review*, Vol. XLVI, September 21, 1963, pp. 49–51.

Woodring, Paul. "Conant's Report Stirs Educators." *The New York Times*, January 16, 1964, p. 73.

Index